By Bradford Fitch

Citizen's Handbook

To Influencing Elected Officials

Citizen Advocacy in State Legislatures and Congress

A Guide for Citizen Lobbyists and Grassroots Advocates

TheCapitol.Net
Alexandria, VA

For over 30 years, TheCapitol.Net and its predecessor, Congressional Quarterly Executive Conferences, have been training professionals from government, military, business, and NGOs on the dynamics and operations of the legislative and executive branches and how to work with them.

Our training and publications include congressional operations, legislative and budget process, communication and advocacy, media and public relations, research, business etiquette, and more.

TheCapitol.Net is a non-partisan firm.

Our publications and courses, written and taught by *current* Washington insiders who are all independent subject matter experts, show how Washington works.™ Our products and services can be found on our web site at *<www.TheCapitol.Net>*.

Additional copies of *Citizen's Handbook To Influencing Elected Officials* can be ordered from your favorite bookseller or online: *<www.TCNCH.com>*.

A condensed version of this book is available for organizations sponsoring Capitol Hill Days/National Advocacy Days. See *<www.PocketGuideToAdvocacy.com>* for information about the *Pocket Guide To Advocacy on Capitol Hill*.

Design and production by Zaccarine Design, Inc., Evanston, IL; 847-864-3994.

∞ The paper used in this publication exceeds the requirements of the American National Standard for Information Sciences—Permanence of Paper for Printed Library Materials, ANSI Z39.48-1992.

v 1

Citizen's Handbook To Influencing Elected Officials
Softcover: ISBN: 1-58733-181-0   Ebook: EISBN: 1-58733-232-9
          ISBN 13: 978-1-58733-181-7   ISBN 13: 978-1-58733-232-6

Table of Contents

Part II:
How to Influence a Legislator 35

About This Book

This book is one part research studies, one part interviews and focus groups, and one part experience. It uses available research on Congress and its decision-making, including studies conducted by the Congressional Management Foundation. Dozens of members of Congress and staff agreed to off-the-record interviews and allowed the author to dissect the factors that contribute to their decisionmaking process. Finally, as a congressional staffer and consultant, the author witnessed or participated in thousands of decisions legislators made in the legislative process. To ensure the confidentiality of those providing insights for this book, most references to legislators will not identify the member of Congress and will be of a general nature.

Although much of the language in this book references Congress, the principles set forth apply to elected officials at the federal, state, and local levels, including state legislators.

Introduction

"We do not have a government of the majority. We have a government of the majority who participate." That statement by Thomas Jefferson reminds us that legislative outcomes in a democracy are not random events. It affirms the belief that, if citizens participate in the democratic process, their voices can make a difference. And it promotes the noble democratic ideals and structures established by the founding fathers, and the proposition that our voice can improve the human condition.

But over the decades Americans have come to believe their voices do not make a difference. Tales of influence-peddling, media stories focusing on corruption, combined with movies' and TV shows' portrayals of Congress have reinforced the notion that "special interests" control Washington. The 2006 scandal involving lobbyist Jack Abramoff—who bought legislative favors for clients with trips, gifts, and meals for policy-makers—reinforced the idea that the average citizen is powerless against well-heeled lobbyists. We are told it's a waste of effort to write an email, make a phone call, or attend a town hall meeting. Members of Congress themselves on the campaign trail perpetuate the notion that Washington is corrupt. "Just elect *me* and I'll fix the problem," they proclaim. It seems the real agenda is set in a smoky backroom by special interest fat-cats and self-interested legislators, and the citizen's opinion isn't worth the few pennies it costs to make a long-distance phone call to a congressman's office.

Here's the truth: they're wrong and Thomas Jefferson was right. Citizens who participate in the democratic process are overwhelmingly the most influential component in any lawmaker's decision-making process. Lunches with lobbyists may occur every day in Washington, and narrow interests occasionally succeed at achieving legislative goals that do not seem to be in the public interest. However, *most* of the factors that make up the congressional agenda, *most* of the legislation that is eventually passed by Congress, and nearly all individual decisions made by members of Congress are directly influenced by citizens who participate. People writing letters, sending emails, attending town hall meetings, visiting lawmakers—they are the dominant influence to legislative outcomes.

This idea may fly in the face of popular belief, but this book will show, with surveys of staff, individual interviews with legislators and staff, and an examination of the actual decisionmaking processes, that the dominant influential factors to legislative outcomes come from citizens. During the course of researching this book, the author was given unprecedented access to legislators and staff, who offered candid off-the-record insights into legislative decision-making. This research shows a process quite different from the one portrayed in popular media.

The key to this conclusion is not found in the front-page headlines of congressional activity, it's found in the day-to-day drudgery of congressional work. What most Americans (and journalists) see is only a fraction of the work and decisions Congress engages in. Journalistic legend Edward R. Murrow described the media as a searching spotlight, focusing on a tiny interesting object for a brief moment, only to move away moments later. The perception may be that Congress is influenced by "special interests," but that perception is based mostly on what the searching spotlight focuses upon. Few reporters or researchers have been given the access to legislators and congressional staff to view the *totality* of legislators' decisionmaking processes.

Very few of legislators' decisions to vote for or against legislation, to cosponsor a bill, or to offer an amendment at a committee hearing, garners a whit of attention—except to a group of constituents in the legislator's state or district. Most of the questions legislators face are *not* the major issues of the day. Members of Congress and staff struggle with hundreds of issues each week that do not affect life-and-death, war-and-peace issues. Should Congress impose a ban on transporting horses in double-decker trailers? Should funding for hospice care for the elderly be increased, and if so, what should be cut to pay for it? Should the ethanol blend levels in gasoline be increased from 10 percent to 15 percent? Such questions are typical of a legislator's work day.

While the media show a Washington where men and women struggle with complex problems—and indeed they do—what you don't see are the less titanic questions that make up most of the work of Congress. These issues are of particular interest to groups of citizens because they affect their livelihood or represent a cause they believe in. And most of the lobbying dollars, constituent visits, and legislative haggling revolve around these kinds of issues that rarely make it into your local newspaper or onto a national TV news show.

Nonetheless, getting involved politically can be a bit intimidating. It's hard to stand up at a town hall meeting in front of your neighbors and tell a member of Congress or state legislator what you think. That is why this book offers practical guidance on how to prepare for a meeting with a legislator, how to write letters and emails to legislators, what is the most effective way to influence legislative staff, and how to write letters to the editor that get noticed by legislators.

Once you recognize that most of the decisions legislators make are not front-page news, yet still have a profound impact on your lives; once you see that those decisions are not influenced by lobbyists and "special interests," but by regular citizens; once you master the basic—but crucial—skills to influence undecided lawmakers, you will be ready to *participate* in the most important conversation humankind ever conceived: the democratic dialogue. This book will show you how.

Part I

How Government Really Works

"In a republic, it is not the people themselves who make the decisions, but the people they themselves choose to stand in their places."

—James Madison

Chapter I

How Congressional Offices Work

In any attempt to influence a group of people it is important to understand their environment. The congressional and state legislative environments are different than other workplaces, and those who appreciate their special characteristics are most successful at their legislative goals.

Citizen-advocates frequently make the mistake of looking at legislatures through the prism of their own work environment: business owners envision Congress as a business, teachers think it must be like a school, and doctors think it works like a hospital. It is natural to apply your own lessons from the work world in an advocacy setting, but it is sometimes detrimental to your cause. It is true that Capitol Hill often resembles a group of independently operating small businesses, the hierarchical nature of the institution feels like a high school, and the rush of activity is similar to an emergency room. Yet the overall environment and the way things get done are unique in our nation. Understanding that environment is vital to winning in the legislative process.

1.1 Dominant Role of Constituents

Constituents drive nearly all decision-making in congressional offices. "I prioritize everything based on anything that's connected to constituents," said one Republican lawmaker. "I want feedback from the real world," he said. Our system of government is set up in such a way that legislators are beholden first and foremost to the people they represent. The House and Senate rules reinforce this connection by legally prohibiting members of Congress from spending office money on behalf of non-constituents.

There are two types of constituents who interact with legislators: those with an *interest* and those with an *opinion*. If a woman stands up at a town hall meeting and says, "I think we should get our troops out of Afghanistan," the congressman will file that in one part of his brain. But if the same woman says, "I think we should get our troops out of Afghanistan because my son is stationed there," the congressman files it in a completely different compartment. The woman has a much stronger bond to the legislator, and he has a much greater obligation to integrate her concerns into his decision-making. Ironically, advocates tend to be more passionate about those issues in which they don't have an interest, but about which they feel strongly. You see much more emotion in letters to Congress from People for the Ethical Treatment of Animals (PETA) about the treatment of baby seals than you do from the American Medical Association (AMA) members concerned about Medicare reimbursement rates.

Traditionally, members of Congress rarely accept meetings with non-constituents or answer mail from outside their district or state. This might frustrate groups who want to influence someone who does not have a constituent-connection to their organization, but their beef is with the founding fathers who set up our system of government. If you want to influence a member of Congress who does not represent you, the best course of action is to get *your* legislator to influence him. If she won't do it, then vote her out of office. (There *are* some methods for influencing legislators who don't represent you, and they are reviewed in § 5.6 on page 43.)

When setting a legislator's daily agenda, constituents always figure prominently. Any constituent who makes the effort to travel to Washington almost always will get a meeting with a member of Congress or his staff. One freshman lawmaker from the West Coast actually established a personal policy of meeting with *every* constituent who traveled to Washington—but had to abandon the policy after a few months because he was shirking his legislative duties. Every constituent who writes their own letter or email to Congress will almost surely get some kind of response, and their message will be integrated into the decisionmaking process in some way. Meetings in the district or state, town hall meetings, and chance encounters on the street are all incredibly influential to legislators, as they know that their very employment is dependent upon understanding their constituents' views. One Republican Senator said, "I have told paid lobbyists for years that any lobbyist worth his salt will concentrate on getting my constituents to tell me what they think . . . not what he thinks. He better spend his time getting them to write me because that's who I listen to." Indeed, members of Congress are experts at gauging public opinion and are the best pollsters of their constituents—as they're the only pollsters who lose their jobs if they get the answer wrong.

1.2 Offices Are Like Small Businesses

Legislator offices are not alike. In fact, Congress is actually an amalgamation of 541[1] small businesses, not a monolithic institution. Each office has the same burdens and challenges of a small business: each one is given a budget, hires employees, purchases equipment and furniture, finds office space, and provides services to customers (constituents). But because they're a part of the government, the managers of these businesses (members of Congress, chiefs of staff, and office managers) confront all of the challenges of running a small business combined with all of the red tape of a bureaucracy. For example, while they have to buy their own computers (there are no bulk sales or discounts available), they also have to comply with various regulations and fill out various forms typical of a bureaucracy.

Each office is given a budget for the year. House offices are allocated about $1.4 million; Senate budgets are larger and vary depending upon the size of the state. Most of this money goes to hiring staff. House offices are limited to 18 full-time people and four part-time people; Senate offices vary and can have 25–100 people on staff. Both institutions have support offices and staffs, such as operational teams that assist individual member offices with phone installation, computers, furniture, etc.

This "independent" office system leads to different degrees of ef-

---

1. Congress is made up of 100 Senators, 435 Representatives, and 6 non-voting Delegates. Delegates are not able to vote on the House floor, but exercise full rights in committees—often making them more powerful than junior House members with floor privileges.

ficiencies and effectiveness. For example, one senior House member has repeatedly overspent his office budget. House office budget rules, which wisely incentivize thriftiness, force him to personally reimburse the government for the overage. And yet this same member chairs an important committee. Some members are well known as horrible managers and bosses. One senator was consistently voted by staff in a survey conducted by *Washingtonian Magazine* as the worst boss on Capitol Hill. And yet he was also widely respected in Congress as a voice of moderation and was elected to the Senate five times.

For the citizen-advocate, the corresponding variance in "customer service" can be quite relevant. If a legislator is not adept at answering his mail and integrating it into his decisionmaking process, then in-person meetings and raising questions at town hall meetings will be more influential. But if a legislator has a solid system for analyzing public opinion based on constituent email, launching a targeted email campaign with an action alert could produce the desired effect.

Congressional offices are divided into two types: *personal* offices (supporting the individual members of Congress) and *committee* offices (supporting committee work). Most of the lobbying and advocacy is directed to legislators' personal offices. The organization of congressional personal offices has evolved during the Congress' 220-plus-year history. The modern system came into existence in the 1970s, and has not changed much from that structure. Offices have two responsibilities: *legislative* and *representational*. These responsibilities are usually divided between two types of offices: the Washington office (legislative) and the district or state office (representational).

The legislative work is what most people read about: writing laws, sitting in committee hearings, and voting on bills. Members and their staff debate the issues of the day, try to develop solutions to societal problems, and it all plays out on the grand stages of the House and Senate. While legislative work gets the most attention, it represents less than half of the labor invested by a personal office.

1.3 Representational Work for Constituents

Most congressional personal office resources and personnel are dedicated to representational duties. This work mostly is in response to individual constituent's questions and requests, and primarily involves two functions: casework and answering constituent mail. "Casework" is the term used in Congress to describe individual requests from constituents for the legislator to intervene on their behalf with a government agency. The requests range from helping a senior citizen get a Social Security check that's been lost in the mail, to aiding a disabled worker in getting his worker's compensation. By far the dominant casework request relates to constituent problems with immigration. Even in offices that are far from the southern border, immigration casework requests can make up a third of the work of congressional district offices. Requests for last-minute passports, green cards to avoid deportation, and educational visas are common.

The Washington office of a member of Congress also spends a great deal of time on another representational duty: answering mail. "Mail" means any kind of constituent communication by letter, fax, postcard, petition, phone call, or email. House offices can get 3,000–5,000 communications a month; Senate offices can range in the tens of thousands, depending upon the size of the state. Staff sort and process these opinions, pleas, and criticisms as best they can. In most House offices there is one junior staffer who sorts the mail and drafts answers to some of it. The rest of it is doled out to two or three legislative assistants. The draft answers are usually reviewed by a legislative director and chief of staff. New language articulating anything related to policy is reviewed by the member herself. In the Senate more people are involved, but the workflow is similar. Legislators are often given summary reports that indicate which issues or positions are getting the most mail. Some freshmen legislators actually try to read every letter going in and out of the office, but this quickly becomes unmanageable. Instead, lawmakers set up a process to integrate the communications into the decisionmaking process, either through tally reports or batches of letters that aptly articulate constituents' views on an issue. (For more on what kind of mail legislators really read, see § 7.2, page 59.)

1.4 Legislative Work for the District, State, and Nation

On the legislative side, member personal offices are little research factories. They collect information, cull for relevant data, and produce output in the form of legislative bills, letters, and press releases. The staff attend hearings, draft statements, summarize reports, and produce memos to the legislator. When approaching a decision the legislator will always consult his staff expert on the topic and usually follow the recommendation of staff. This does not mean that staff control all decision-making; they do not. Rather, it means that staff are usually in tune with the thinking of their bosses, and guide them to a decision they assume the legislator desires.

Legislative staff are both research assistants and policy advisors to members of Congress. They research the facts of an issue, collect the positions of interested parties, analyze the implications to constituents, and synthesize the information for legislators. Legislative assistants (known as LA's) also interject recommendations on policy decisions on almost every issue in their portfolios and research memos. They become policy experts, no matter how limited their experience with the issue, and pride themselves on their ability to influence legislators.

Chapter 2

Congressional Culture

Jack McIver Weatherford's 1985 book, *Tribes on the Hill*, divided up the Congress using anthropological terms, which is an apt way of looking at the culture and environment. Congress is a balance of tribes: the youthful staff toiling in offices, the optimistic freshman members who believe *their* generation will be the one to push aside partisan disagreement, the cynical reporters seeking to make a name for themselves by criticizing any minor misstep and spotlighting any flaw, and the crusty old lion senators who contemplate legislation like Roman counsels and fill the Senate chamber with rhetoric. This mix results in a strange and dynamic clash of old and new, fury and calm, together propagating a type of political weather pattern that suggests simultaneously that anything is possible but little can be accomplished.

2.1 Working Environment of Congress

The work schedule is brutal. Fifty hours a week is common—60 to 70 hours a week is the norm in the final days leading up to a congressional recess. Congressional leaders for years have sought to change the phrase "Congressional Recess" to "District Work Period," as the word "recess" conjures up images of legislators frolicking about, playing kickball and goofing off. In fact, when members of Congress are home their schedules are packed with 10-hour days of constituent meetings, public events, speeches and other district-oriented activities.

The working environment for staff is not how it is portrayed on television. The work is fast-paced, but sometimes mundane, and the Washington offices are cramped. Basic workplace safety laws didn't even apply to congressional employees until 1995, when Congress passed the Congressional Accountability Act. Now Congress must comply with a series of worker protection laws, such as the Civil Rights Act and the Fair Labor Standards Act. Congress had such a poor reputation for working conditions it was often referred to in the 1980s as "The Last Plantation."

Quarters are so cramped that offices sometimes create work spaces in rooms designed for storage. So, if you walk up to the fifth floor of the Cannon House Office Building, don't be surprised if you see interns working in what appear to be storage cages. This practice has fallen out of favor in recent years, but the pressure to produce reams of work has not abated. Congress feels it cannot add more staff or create new office buildings for fear it would be accused of "spending money on itself." The number of staff that a House member is allotted by law has not changed since 1979, despite the fact that the workload has grown exponentially.

2.2 Congressional Hierarchy

The House is like a high school, with freshman legislators seeking to make an impression, aggressive subcommittee chairmen looking for angles to reach leadership levels, and senior members ruling on the most important matters. Each House member is looking for their own niche issue: a legislative topic where they can become an expert, introduce bills, and become the source for reporters. Subcommittee and committee chairmen act as the gatekeepers who determine, with the leadership's input, the flow of legislation to the House floor.

The Senate is often called "the world's most exclusive club." Even the Senate Majority Leader, who is the most powerful member of the institution, recognizes that a single senator can derail any legislative initiative. Senate rules allow each member virtually unlimited time for debate and the unrestricted ability to offer amendments to legislation. Allowing the Senate to take its time reviewing pending legislation to ensure it would benefit the nation was the founding fathers' way of balancing the hot and sudden passions of the House.

2.3 Committees—
Where the Real Work Is Done

Otto Von Bismarck, the 19th Century German chancellor, said, "If you like laws or sausages, don't watch how either are made." Congressional committees are the great sausage factories of the legislative process. They are where our elected officials merge language, law, hope, inspiration, anger, compassion, constituent and party pressure, and their personal views of human nature and society into the rules that we must abide by. Committees engage in three basic activities: 1) conduct legislative hearings on bills; 2) conduct oversight of the executive branch and societal institutions; 3) and amend and vote on bills.

Capitol Hill legislative hearings have become stages for theater (some might say bad theater) as much as they are components of the legislative process. One committee staff director said, "Conducting a hearing is like directing a play. You write your script, pick your cast, and hope the audience likes it." Hearings allow legislators to gather information on pending legislation or issues, provide a forum for experts and interested parties to voice their knowledge or concern, and allow legislators to probe into the impact of one policy or another on the nation.

Oversight hearings are much like legislative hearings in form except that there need not be a specific bill discussed or even the potential for legislation offered. While the Constitution offers no explicit language on Congress' oversight role, the founding fathers recognized that a system of checks and balances wasn't merely about debating individual legislative proposals—the Congress could exercise its power simply by examining and questioning the performance of the President and executive branch in the process of identifying cures to public ills. Examples include Sen. Joe McCarthy's investigation into communism in the early 1950s, the Watergate hearings of the 1970s, and the Iran-Contra hearings of the late 1980s. These have acted as templates for legislators and staff who seek to right some wrong through public exposure. As Supreme Court Justice Louis Brandeis said, "Sunlight is said to be the best disinfectant."

Finally, while oversight hearings may be the best congressional theater, the process of amending and passing legislation in congressional committees is more workman-like. It is the legislative process at its core—people offering ideas, debating with colleagues, and compromising to accomplish the achievable.

The meeting starts with a proposed bill and the process is called a "markup" (literally meaning to "mark up" the document). Committee members have the opportunity to offer amendments to the bill. The language may be in legalese, but someone is always around to translate it into English, and most legislators have a firm understanding of what they're voting on. Each amendment is voted up or down, or adopted by "voice vote"—meaning there was no recorded vote and it was unanimously passed. The subcommittee or committee chairman looms large over all committee bill amendment processes. He controls the agenda, chooses the order of amendments to be considered, and has the option to offer a complete substitute to the scheduled bill (called the "chairman's mark"). Plus, any committee member knows that they oppose the chairman at their own peril, as opposition to a chairman's pet bill may well result in becoming an outcast—a legislator whose legislation is never considered by his committee.

2.4 Congressional Staff Descriptions

Here is the breakdown of the standard congressional office.

- ### Chief of Staff

  This is the head honcho in any congressional office. The person is usually the closest advisor to the legislator and perhaps a long-time personal friend. They run the operation much like a chief operations officer. (Up until the 1990s this position was known as "Administrative Assistant.")

- ### State/District Director

  The top congressional staffer in the state or district, and the manager of the operations of the state/district offices. This person usually has the best on-the-ground political skills, and may be a former campaign operative. She oversees the legislator's in-state/district schedule, and is likely the primary liaison to the groups and individuals key to the legislator's re-election.

• Legislative Director

This staffer, called the "LD," is the senior policy staffer in the office. She likely has been with the office for more than three or four years, promoted from legislative assistant, and oversees all major policy decisions. She likely oversees and edits all new letters/emails drafted by more junior staffers, and has jurisdiction over the issues most important to the legislator or the most prominent issues as determined by the legislator's committee assignments.

• Legislative Assistant

This staffer, called an "LA," is the primary office expert on a particular issue. He drafts statements and speeches, writes memos on legislation, and advises the legislator on the issues in her jurisdiction. In the House, LA's can have up to 15 issues to follow; the jurisdiction of Senate LA's ranges from one to 10 issues, depending upon the size of the office. House LA's tend to be younger (under 30), while in the Senate they tend to be older and have graduate degrees. Those who stick around awhile merit "title-bumps" and get rewarded for not leaving the office—in the House these staffers are called "Senior Legislative Assistants," and in the Senate they may gain the title of "Legislative Counsel."

• Legislative Correspondent

This staffer, called an "LC", is primarily responsible for managing and drafting responses to mail. Typically they are very young (under 25) and have less than two years of experience on the Hill. They toil at this thankless job, sorting thousands of emails, faxes, postcards, and letters each month, with the hope that they'll get promoted after one of the LA's finds another job. LC's are often assigned non-controversial issues so they can gain some experience working directly with constituents. If you're visiting Washington, and the title of the aide you meet with is "Legislative Correspondent," it means it's a very busy day and the LA with jurisdiction had a scheduling conflict.

• Systems Administrator

This staffer is responsible for the office's information technology. The Systems Administrator also may have some mail management responsibility. They usually trouble-shoot problems with the computer systems, provide reports to senior staff and the legislator on "mail counts" (who's writing on what), and liaison with institutional offices to ensure the office is up to speed with technological developments and requirements.

• Staff Assistant

This staffer primarily handles phone calls to the office and greets visitors. Wise legislators hire someone from the district or state for this job in their Washington office, so that callers feel an instant connection. They are often straight out of college and usually former congressional interns. They also handle requests to purchase American flags that have been flown over the U.S. Capitol (a commercial custom still practiced in Congress) and often oversee interns. If you find yourself visiting Washington or calling on an issue, be careful how you treat them—today's staff assistant is tomorrow's chief of staff, and one former House staff assistant became a U.S. senator.

• Scheduler

This staffer may also share the title of Office Manager, and is responsible for the legislator's schedule. Some lawmakers have two schedulers—one in DC and another in the state/district. The scheduler is the ultimate gatekeeper and may be the person who determines whether you and your group meets with a legislator. (In the House, the chief of staff may be the decision-maker, but some Senate schedulers are known to make even chiefs of staff cower.)

• Caseworker/Field Representative

This staffer's primary responsibility is to respond to requests from constituents and to act as a liaison or advocate in solving some problem, usually involving a federal agency. Each office has an elaborate system for reviewing and tracking these requests. The caseworker usually has a network of contacts with federal agencies that allows her to cut through red tape. These staffers also may attend functions or events on behalf of the legislator, representing the member of Congress, conveying her position on issues important to the group, and relaying back information on the event to the legislator and staff.

• Press Secretary/Communications Director

This staffer is responsible for the legislator's public relations. House offices usually have one person dedicated to the job, while Senate offices can have up to five, depending upon the size of the state. Press secretaries write press releases, liaise with reporters, oversee the web site and social media, draft some speeches, and advise the legislator on the public relations impact of decisions.

• Intern

It is disappointing when a young person is asked by a constituent what he does in the office and he replies, "I'm just an intern." The reality is that Capitol Hill would surely grind to a halt without the thousands of people who comprise this enthusiastic and free labor force. Interns open the mail, answer the phones, conduct guided tours of the Capitol building for constituent groups, and sometimes even cover hearings. I conducted dozens of intern training programs for the House of Representatives, and each time when I was about to cast out these fresh young souls to three months of administrative servitude, I reminded them they didn't have to be "just an intern" . . . and told them this story.

In 2001 Jennifer Luciano was an intern for Congressman Danny Davis (D-IL). While conducting constituent tours of the U.S. Capitol Building she noticed that there were no statues recognizing the role of African-American women in the suffragette movement. Jennifer noted this absence to Congressman Davis' chief of staff, who in turn passed it on to the congressman, who said, "You're right, we ought to do something about this." So, on June 20, 2001, with her grandfather and mother in attendance, Jennifer was recognized at a press conference on the grounds of the U.S. Capitol as Congressman Danny Davis introduced H. Con. Res 169, "Directing the Architect of the Capitol to enter into a contract for the design and construction of a monument to commemorate the contributions of minority women to women's suffrage and to the participation of women in public life, and for other purposes." Eight years later a statue of the African-American suffragette, Sojourner Truth, took its place beside Washington, Jackson, and Jefferson. Being "just an intern" sometimes means more than opening the mail.

Chapter 3

How Legislators
Make Decisions

Despite the efforts of high school social studies teachers, parents, journalists, and political scientists, our governmental process is a mystery to most Americans. More Americans can name all of the *Three Stooges* than can name a member of the U.S. Supreme Court. Caricatures, misconceptions, and stereotypes dominate citizens' view of the Congress, which contribute to our reluctance to more fully participate. In reality, the system works pretty much as we were taught in the third grade.

By design the American Congress is slow and deliberative. The founding fathers' creation was in reaction to an 18th century monarchy that was quick to impose authoritarian rule on the colonists, often with unpleasant effects. So the new government in 1789 was set up with an elaborate system of checks and balances, ensuring that no branch or section of government could dominate the process or the citizen. While this is at times frustrating, it is the fundamental reason why the United States has endured for more than 200 years (while many other governments have not).

Individual legislators must wrestle with this deliberative system, and meld their own beliefs with political pressures into a legislative melting pot that hopefully results in a positive societal outcome. Legislators use a kind of political math to make decisions, weighing a variety of factors when determining whether to vote for or against a bill, to cosponsor legislation, or to support or oppose funding for an initiative. When all the details are burned away, legislators follow three voices when making a decision. One member of Congress called these voices the "Three H's": Heart, Head, and Health (political health).

3.1 Heart

People who make decisions that affect the lives and well-being of others are usually first guided by their own beliefs and value system. When asked how he made decisions, a GOP House lawmaker said, "I'm guided by the values my parents taught me. What's the most common-sense, ethical way to solve the problem?" Legislators genuinely grapple with difficult decisions that affect every aspect of our lives.

There is no directory that lists which legislators are mostly guided by their conscience and which are motivated by other factors. Generally, senators, who enjoy six-year terms, are expected to demonstrate a "leadership" method of decision-making, sometimes bucking public opinion. This is the way the system was designed. The Senate is supposed to be a more deliberative, thoughtful institution and intended to be a check on the House, which could be swayed by the hot passions of the public. This general rule about the Senate tends to fade the closer the senator gets to re-election (funny how that works). And in the House, more senior members who are in "safe" seats with little danger of losing re-election are more inclined to follow their own counsel rather than other factors.

3.2 Head

Working in the Congress is a policy wonk's dream. You have access to *every* study every written, every expert in the country, every federal, state, and local agency. And if that's not enough, the largest library in the world—the Library of Congress—is across the street from your office. Most legislators and staff *love* doing research on public policy problems. This is why they chose this career—to analyze difficult issues and develop an approach or solution to improve the human condition.

Legislators are constantly hunting for unbiased, independent research to help them make a decision. There is both a practical and political reason for this: in addition to guiding their thinking, independent studies that justify a policy also provide them some political cover. A member of Congress told me that he had changed his position on the issue of global warming/climate change, from being opposed to mandatory caps on emissions to being in favor of them. Since he represented a coal-producing district, when he was asked what contributed to his change in thinking, he said, "I read the 300-

page United Nations study on the topic." Many legislators are policy wonks—that's the real reason they run for public office. They study issues, interpret data, and determine the best public policy based on their analysis. One member of Congress had a "to read" pile that was *four feet high*. She would often forgo sleep ("Four hours a night is OK sometimes," she would say) in order to gain complete understanding of an issue.

3.3 Health (political)

Politics is often considered a dirty word, and yet what citizens and pundits fail to realize is that when a legislator factors "politics" into making a decision, it often means that the legislator is *listening to constituents*. Usually a legislator's personal beliefs and the general attitudes of his constituency are not far apart—that's why she got elected. Yet most decisions don't affect a majority of the citizenry in a district or state; they tend to impact small groups in significant ways. For example, Medicare reimbursement rates primarily impact doctors, research funding on a particular disease affects those afflicted with the illness, and immigration visa limits on hiring high-tech, non-citizen workers tend to concern technology companies.

There may be other major issues of the day, such as the war in Iraq or climate change, that engender opinions in nearly everyone. But those issues are rare in the day-to-day world of government. Most decisions affect a narrow class of people, which makes the politics fairly easy to assess. When faced with a new issue, one House chief of staff said he first asks, "Who's for it, who's against it?"

There are many ways legislators assess the political impact of a decision. Yet for nearly every decision each legislator will conduct a personal political analysis of how it impacts voters' perceptions in his district or state and how it might affect his next election. It's important to note that even legislators in safe districts are very much swayed by constituents' views. This is for two reasons. First, they feel an ethical responsibility to honestly represent the people who elected them (it sounds corny, but they do). Second, politicians want to be loved by everyone—that's part of the reason they went into politics. For better or worse, legislators sometimes measure their self-worth by their election margin—and anything that could drop them below 60 percent re-election rate will give them heartburn. A legislator told me, "I sometimes think that every member of Congress is a middle child still trying to please his father."

The notion that legislators are guided by these three factors— heart, head, and health—defies the popular (albeit cynical) belief that other influences are the "real" reason behind legislative behavior. However, both anecdotal and survey research support this conclusion. In 2004 and 2005, the Congressional Management Foundation conducted the most extensive survey ever done of congressional staff, including more than 350 policy and communications staff in more than 200 offices. According to staff, the factors that most influenced an undecided legislator were, in this order: 1) constituent meetings; 2) personally written letters and emails, and; 3) anyone who represents a constituent (such as a union leader, state association president, or large employer). (See Chart 1, page 34.)

This collision of cynical popular belief and reality became clear to me in the most surprising setting: talking to congressional interns. During my 13 years on Capitol Hill I always supervised the interns in the office. And at the end of their three-month tenure, I always asked the same question: "What belief or stereotype about Washington and Congress was debunked during your time here?" The most common answer went something like this: "I was surprised at how much you people wrestle with trying to figure out the right thing to do, and how much you worry about the impact of your decisions on constituents." If you spend a little time in the real Washington—not the one you see on the front pages or in the movies—you'll come to the same conclusion.

Finally, any analysis of what goes into legislative decision-making would be incomplete without addressing a prevalent belief in our society: members of Congress don't know what's in the bills they vote on. While it is true the rare provision helping one group or another can be tucked into massive bills without most legislators' or staff knowledge, members of Congress are amply educated on what they're voting on. They usually don't read the legislative language (they have lawyers to do that). Instead, they read accurate detailed summaries or other reports created by a vast army of researchers working both in and out of Congress. It's nonsense to think that political creatures whose professional survival is dependent on how their votes are interpreted are going to guess their way through it. Members of Congress take pains to know exactly what they're doing when they vote "yea" or "nay" on any bill before them.

Chapter 4

People Who Can (and Can't) Influence Legislators and How They Do It

As noted throughout this book, constituents usually dominate legislator's decision-making. But just as you would consult multiple sources before making a big decision, members of Congress do the same thing. They consult family, friends, people they work with, and experts on the topic.

4.1 Family and Friends Have the Lawmaker's Ear

Legislators are like everyone else—when they have a tough decision to make they talk to the people they trust most: spouses, parents, colleagues, and friends. In the 2008 Democratic primary battle between Senators Hillary Clinton and Barack Obama, Senator Bob Casey of Pennsylvania said that a factor in his decision to endorse Obama was pressure from his four daughters. They don't have to be experts on a topic to have influence. They just have to have the ear of a member of Congress and be someone he trusts.

4.2 Knowledgeable Acquaintances Can Make a Difference

Legislators know a *lot* of people. Some folks claim to be "a friend of the congressman" when they saw him once at some charity event. Regardless of the depth of the relationship, many people can get the ear of a member of Congress. (One lawmaker estimated that 2,000 people had his personal cell phone number. He spent a lot of time answering his cell phone.) If these acquaintances have knowledge of a particular topic they can be very influential, as they may be tagged "expert" and "friend" by the member of Congress—a powerful combination. "What also really works is when I get calls from individual supporters that I know and respect," said one senator. "They'll call me and say, 'I've known you for years and I know this issue.' I listen to that."

4.3 Legislators Pay Attention to Respected Colleagues

There was a freshmen member of Congress who, when confronted with a tough decision on military matters, would ask, "How is Les Aspin voting on this?" Congressman Aspin was the Chairman of the Armed Services Committee (1985–1993) and later served as Secretary of Defense under President Clinton. Sometimes legislators seek guidance from expert legislators who have studied an issue and bring a politician's perspective to the debate. Junior members of a congressional delegation may wait to see how the "dean of the delegation" (the state's most senior member) will vote before determining their position. And rarely, members of Congress will have no idea how they're going to vote on an issue until they walk onto the House floor and observe how an influential colleague has just voted.

4.4 Legislative Leaders and Arm Twisting

All members of Congress are subject to pressure from fellow legislators in the leadership hierarchy of the institution. Members of the House of Representatives are much more susceptible to influence than senators because House rules allow leadership to set the agenda and the Senate affords more power to individual senators. Stories of last-minute arm twisting are legendary and have changed the outcomes of many votes. Former House Majority Leader Tom DeLay (R-TX) earned the nickname "The Hammer" as a result of his tactics. He once held a vote open for four hours (in violation of House Rules) in order to turn one or two "no" votes into "yeas." It may be the persuasiveness of the argument, or the presence of power that sways opinions, but either way it is an influential factor in all legislators' decision-making.

4.5 The Real Influence of Lobbyists

The popular portrayal of lobbyists' influence on governmental decision-making is largely inaccurate. Most lobbyists in Washington don't drive fancy cars, don't have expense accounts, and don't work for fat-cat corporations. Moreover, they rarely determine policy outcomes— organized citizens do. Most lobbyists are professional advocates who believe in their cause and understand the details of an issue, whether it be finding a cure for diabetes, improving the environment, or opposing new taxes that could cause businesses to lay off workers. Most people in Washington who make their livelihoods as professional advocates don't actually work for lobbying firms. They work for associations, nonprofits, and companies representing millions of Americans affiliated with their organization. The influence they wield is not with money. Their power is in their knowledge of a topic, ability to communicate the issue effectively, and accurately interpreting how a policy decision will affect a lawmaker's state or district.

Lobbyists, often former congressional staffers or members of Congress, do trade on their previous relationships to gain access to those in power. But once they get that access, they are armed mostly with the facts surrounding a topic and how it might affect a group of people. Citizens have the same tools as lobbyists—access to their members of Congress and knowledge of how an issue might impact their lives.

The roles and influence of lobbyists was summed up best by Jeffrey H. Birnbaum, formerly of *The Washington Post*, one of the leading reporters on the intersection of special interests and policy-making. He wrote in 2008, "Lobbying is much more substantive and out in the open than its ugly caricature. Lobbyists primarily woo lawmakers with facts. Making the case is what effective lobbyists do most and best. They spend the rest of their time persuading lawmakers' constituents to back the same causes, very much in the mode of an electoral campaign. If members of Congress see merit in a position and there is a public outcry in its favor, that's the way they tend to vote." (*The Washington Post,* "Mickey Goes to Washington," 2/17/08)

4.6 Campaign Contributors Are Less Influential Than You Think

There's a dirty secret in Washington that neither Congress nor the special interest community want out: campaign contributions really don't influence legislative outcomes all that much. The reality is that a campaign contributor will likely get access to a legislator, such as getting a phone call returned by a member of Congress or his senior staff. However, the average constituent can get the same access with about the same amount of effort, such as by showing up at a town hall meeting, or by getting three or four fellow constituents with similar interests to set up an in-person meeting in the legislator's Washington or state office.

A chief of staff was asked to gauge who had more influence: someone who gave his boss $1,000 in campaign contributions, or a constituent who had flown to Washington for a meeting with the congressman. His reply, "About the same—it just depends on who makes the best argument." Also keep in mind that with the skyrocketing costs of campaigns, and the strict limits imposed by new campaign finance laws, a $1,000 contribution represents a tiny fraction of what the lawmaker must raise for his re-election effort. One House member from a competitive district said, "A mistake that critics make is that they overestimate the role of money and underestimate the power of the threat of the next election."

4.7 Are Legislators Driven by Polling?

Legislators read polls about everything: their approval rating, their chances for re-election, the mood of the district, opinions on the priority of issues, and even the exact words that will work best in their campaigns. It varies legislator to legislator as to whether polls influence decision-making. And it also varies from issue to issue. A member of Congress may generally think a trade agreement with another country could be in the best long-term interests of the nation, but if he represents a union-dominated district that is overwhelmingly opposed, he might follow public opinion. In contrast, when legislators make decisions about whether to send the nation to war (which has occurred twice recently, in 1991 and 2003), I don't know of a single member of Congress who didn't search deep in her soul for the right answer and generally ignored public polling. Polls are sometimes singled out as influencing lawmakers' decision-making, and they are used by lawmakers to gauge public opinion (especially near elections). However, they are but one factor that legislators consider.

4.8 How Paid Advertising Affects Legislators' Thinking

Occasionally, interest groups will purchase television, radio, print, or Internet advertising (called "paid media"). There are two categories of advocacy advertising: ads genuinely intended to influence the decision-making of a member of Congress near a crucial vote by swaying public opinion in his state; and ads timed around elections, that look like advocacy messages but which are really intended to influence voters about to go to the polls. Messages of the campaign variety will include numerous attacks on the legislator's opinions, voting record, or character—and conclude with the line, "Send a message to Representative Smith." (The unstated assumption is the "message" is a one-way ticket out of Congress.) These are designed to influence election outcomes rather than policy. Numerous rulings by the U.S. Supreme Court have established that these messages are not covered under federal campaign finance law restrictions, allowing unlimited amount of spending of this kind.

In some legislative battles interested parties will pay for advertising in a legislator's state with the goal of generating a groundswell of support for their position. They hope it will translate into calls, emails, and letters to the congressional office. One of the best examples of this occurred in 1994, when the "Harry and Louise" ads targeted members of Congress vulnerable for re-election. They depicted a typical family in various real-life settings discussing the potential impact of President Clinton's health care reform proposal on the family members. The campaign is credited as a major factor in the defeat of President Clinton's plan. If these campaigns are well done and generate calls and emails to the legislators, they can be factors in influencing legislators.

4.9 You Are Competing with Everyone, Even Though You Don't Know It

When individuals participate in "lobby days" or "fly-ins" to Washington to advocate a particular cause, attendees will often look at their particular issue and say, "This makes perfect sense! Who could oppose this idea?" The answer is, "Everyone!"

Every individual, constituency group, association, corporation, and nonprofit group "petitioning their government for a redress of grievances" is competing with you for the time, attention, and resources of a member of Congress and the U.S. government. Each legislator has a limited amount of energy and political capital they can expend. Every year the federal budget apportions a limited amount of funds to be spent. Each year the subcommittees of the House Appropriations Committee are allotted a set amount of money to spend on particular programs. This allotment is nearly impossible to increase.

When a group meets with a legislator the meeting is likely one of dozens the legislator has that week with similar groups. As legislators and staff assess which proposal or appropriation to support, they are weighing it against hundreds of other requests for support. In order to stand out you must distinguish your cause in some manner, or a competing group will win the limited attention, resources, and support each legislator possesses.

The next chapter will show you how to do it.

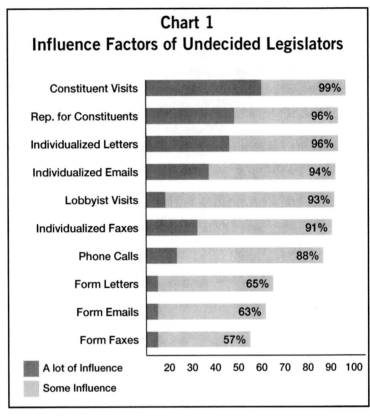

**Chart 1
Influence Factors of Undecided Legislators**

Constituent Visits	99%
Rep. for Constituents	96%
Individualized Letters	96%
Individualized Emails	94%
Lobbyist Visits	93%
Individualized Faxes	91%
Phone Calls	88%
Form Letters	65%
Form Emails	63%
Form Faxes	57%

■ A lot of Influence   20 30 40 50 60 70 80 90 100
☐ Some Influence

This chart depicts the answer to the following question posed in two Congressional Management Foundation surveys of more than 350 congressional staffers conducted in 2004 and 2005:

"If your Member/Senator has not already arrived at a firm decision on an issue, how much influence might the following advocacy strategies directed to the Washington office have on his/her decision?"

Part II

How to Influence a Legislator

"When I feel the heat, I see the light."

—Senator Everett Dirksen (R-Illinois,
Senate Minority Leader, 1959–1969)

The Introduction of this book offers some lofty democratic ideals, beckoning readers to appreciate their unrealized strength as citizen-advocates, and to use that power for some societal good. It's a little like the speech Vince Lombardi would give to his team on the first day of spring training. Part II *is* spring training (without the wind sprints). All the passion in the world can't move a mountain without the right tools and people who know how to use them.

This Part includes overarching strategies for constituents to influence legislators; how to best influence legislators and their staff in face-to-face interactions; and best practices for communications to Congress and state legislatures.

Chapter 5

Strategies for Influencing Legislators

5.1 Get to Them BEFORE They Take a Stand

The most important rule for influencing a legislator has to do with timing. If a member of Congress or a state legislator already has come to a decision, you will have a difficult time changing his position. Politicians learn early on in their careers that there is a huge price to pay for inconsistency. Reporters and opponents will crucify them as "flip-floppers" if they change a position. Therefore, once they take a position on an issue, they'll stick to it.

Congressman Mo Udall (D-AZ) told a wonderful joke about politicians' and journalists' obsession with consistency. He said, "If I killed my mother, the media wouldn't attack me for committing murder. They would point out that I advocated against matricide in my last campaign." This doesn't mean it is impossible to turn a "no" into a "yes," and this book outlines ways to do it. It merely suggests that it is *much* easier to turn an "undecided" into a "yes."

5.2 The Personal Story Trumps All

It is impossible to overstate the importance of constituents' personal stories and the influence they have in the policy process. Legislators trying to determine the best policy outcome can wrestle with facts and figures until they are bleary-eyed. And yet, when they come face-to-face with an actual person whom the policy affects, it completely focuses their thinking. They no longer see data and reports associated with that policy; they see a person. And no matter the legislator's position on the issue—pro or con—she feels an obligation to the person: either to help him, or to adequately explain why she can't. "The most effective way to influence a lawmaker is for a constituent to talk to a legislator about how the policy will affect the person or a particular group," said one House Democrat.

If the story is powerful enough, and demonstrates some societal injustice or ill, it may actually be translated into legislation. "Megan's Law" requires law enforcement authorities to make public information regarding sexual offenders. It was enacted because of the powerful story of a little girl who was abducted, raped and killed. There is now a popular trend of naming bills after victims, such as Heather's Law, Rachel's Law, Haley's Act, and the Amber Alert system. On the lighter side, a constituent told a congressman about an unpleasant experience he had at a doctor's office. After being asked to disrobe and to put on a flimsy paper smock, the man was asked to sign papers related to his care without fully understanding their meaning. He felt quite uncomfortable and compromised in the setting, which led the legislator to introduce a bill, "No Private Contracts to Be Negotiated When the Patient is Buck Naked Act."

One House Democrat, who is a member of the powerful House Appropriations Committee, had this experience which demonstrates the value of personal stories. "I went to a luncheon that was hosted by cancer centers in my state," he said. "Instead of having those guys in white coats doing their lobbying, they brought in patients—kids and their parents. They all got up and told their stories. When it was done there wasn't a dry eye in the room. They gave us the human importance of those dollars we were being asked to appropriate. Every group needs to do that."

5.3 How to Build Long-term Relationships with Legislators

The most effective advocates are not the ones who suddenly become interested in an issue. They are the ones who are consistently interested in and demonstrate an expertise about a topic. Here are three tips for building a long-term relationship with a legislator.

1. Learn about your lawmaker

Dale Carnegie taught us years ago that understanding someone else's problems and interests is the best way to "win friends and influence people." Politicians are people too (contrary to what you might have read), and they are susceptible to the same types of influences. An advocate is going to be much more powerful if he starts a conversation by asking about a congressman's kid who just went to college, or mention that he saw her picture in the newspaper recently at a ribbon cutting. Prior to the meeting learn about the bills she's introduced, issues she's spoken out on, and recent legislative accomplishments.

2. Establish yourself as a helpful expert, and offer to be a researcher

The reason that lobbyists are so successful at their job isn't because they take people to lunch, it's because they *know* the issues. The most valuable gift a lobbyist gives a member of Congress isn't a campaign contribution—it's a detailed analysis of how a particular issue affects the lawmaker's district or state. Some state association, nonprofit and corporate leaders offer this data, but many do not. Identify and research how a particular issue affects the legislator's constituents, and she'll call *you* for advice.

3. Communicate frequently

Every congressional office knows those in-district advocates who stay on top of issues and don't hesitate to offer help or advice on how a legislator should vote. Keeping in regular contact with your legislators provides a valuable service to legislators and staff, and keeps them accountable to voters.

5.4 How to Leverage Your Affiliations to Magnify Your Power

If you belong to any group, such as an association, nonprofit, or company, chances are they've asked you to take some kind of action such as calling or emailing your legislators. It may seem like they're annoying you, and you may feel you don't have the time. However, this is the most important service advocacy departments provide supporters. They are monitoring the governmental process in Washington or state capitals and alerting you, "Your interests are at stake!"

Timing is often crucial, sometimes involving quick and unexpected committee votes, so it's essential that advocates respond rapidly and as requested.

Advocacy organizations and departments are also valuable sources of background material on a particular topic. If you're a new advocate and want to get involved in a campaign, an organization's web site usually has a section labeled "advocacy," "public affairs," "legislative action center," "take action," or "governmental affairs." Tap into these resources to build a better understanding of the issue and how it affects you. These sections may also maintain a legislative scorecard, which provides the organization's assessment on how legislators have performed regarding your issues. Lawmakers tend to dislike these scorecards, and they occasionally are unfair. However, anytime a lobbyist tells a member of Congress, "This will be one of the votes we'll include in our annual scorecard," the politician knows he will be held to an additional level of accountability.

Finally, there are a few organized groups that have a powerful voice in our democracy because of their reputation for organizing grassroots efforts in both legislative battles and elections. AARP, the National Rifle Association, and teachers unions all represent the views of millions of Americans. Media critics often confuse this grassroots power with their fund-raising capabilities, suggesting it's "special interest money" that influences lawmakers.

The reality comes down to sheer numbers—people who share a common belief and are willing to put their voice and vote behind that belief. You may disagree with their tactics and policy positions, but democracies are supposed to be responsive to large numbers of voters. One House Democrat from a southern state, referring to a powerful group in his state, summed it up. "Their money is beside the point. They can mobilize and intensify a group of motivated constituents who can put the fear of God in members of Congress."

5.5 How to Map Your Economic and Political Footprint

Every citizen has an economic and political footprint, which represents everything you are and do that interfaces with government. The taxes you pay, employees you hire, club memberships you possess—anything that represents your weight and power as a citizen goes into the equation. Some citizens have a greater economic and political footprint than others, such as union leaders, state association presidents, or CEOs of large companies. These individuals can claim to be the voice of others and command greater attention from elected officials. However, if you genuinely consider the breadth and depth of your world, you'd be surprised at how powerful you would seem to a politician.

Start by considering your home and work. Instantly, you might find yourself represented by two members of Congress if your place of work is in a different congressional district. "But aren't legislators only representing constituents who can vote for them?" Yes, technically that is correct. However, politicians are savvy enough to know that coworkers talk to one another. If he messes up you'll end up talking trash about him next time you're at the water cooler.

Also consider every organization you belong to or are affiliated with. This includes professional associations, clubs, school groups, alumni chapters, and even organizations you give charitable donations to. Every one of these connections gives you an opportunity to expand your political footprint. When you start your letter to a congressman with, "I'm a member of (insert well-known group here)," the legislator doesn't see a single individual, she sees an entire group, and you as their representative voice.

Finally, when all the affiliations are burned away, you might be surprised to learn what category of citizen starts out with a very large political footprint: college students. The organizer of a graduate student group conducting their first lobby day on Capitol Hill asked, "Should we try to set up meetings with legislators who represent our home districts, or where we go to school." The correct reply is "Both!"

U.S. election laws allow college students to register to vote in *either* the state they call home or where they go to school. So, the elected official doesn't *know* where this young person might register, and therefore will always consider the student a potential voter.

5.6 How to Influence Legislators Who Don't Represent You

Citizen-advocates often ask, "How do I influence a legislator who doesn't represent my district?" The short answer is, "You don't." The founding fathers gave us a republic, a representative democracy. We elect those individuals to represent our interests in Washington and state capitals. If they don't do that well, we have the option to vote them out of office.

The only way to influence someone who you don't have the opportunity to vote for is to expand your economic and political footprint. Identify where you might have interests and use that leverage to influence legislators. A business owner may live in District 1, but operate her business in District 2. She is perfectly within her rights as a citizen to send an email to the District 2 congressman with the opening, "I run a flower shop in your district and employ 10 people from your town." You may also play some representational role in an association or group. The leader of a state teachers association did not live in the district that a congressman represented, but that congressman always made time to meet with the association leader because he spoke for an association of 3,000 teachers in our district.

5.7 How to Influence Congressional Committee Staff

Staffers who work in committees differ from those working in members' personal offices in a few ways. They are usually experts in one particular field, and are more likely to be older and have a graduate degree in a related subject. They may have come from the executive branch, providing them with valuable insight into the topics and federal agencies they now oversee. They also may be somewhat bureaucratic in nature, spending decades working on one committee or subcommittee and becoming the preeminent experts on a particular recurring piece of legislation that requires reauthorization every few years.

Prior to the 1990s it was not uncommon for committee staff to retain their jobs even if the Congress changed parties after an election—chairmen valued staff expertise over partisanship. That practice, however, is no longer the norm, and when the electorate decides it's time to vote one party out of power in the House or Senate, thousands of professional committee staff members begin brushing up their resumes.

Staff who work for congressional committees are hard to influence, somewhat reclusive, and among the most powerful people in Washington. Influencing this cadre of people is the most difficult part of the advocacy process. They shield themselves from constituents, resist entreaties from interested parties, and generally hide out from anyone seeking favor. So how do you influence this caste of legislative professionals?

Your entrée to this group is most likely through a professional advocate. If you belong to a nonprofit group or association, it probably employs someone who is hired to build relationships with committee staff. If your story is representative of a particular governmental issue or problem, the person drafting legislation to address the problem will want to hear about it. Ask your group to set up a call or meeting between you and a committee staffer, and make sure your story is heard.

The other way to influence a committee is through another legislator. Some advocates lament that they can't influence congressional committees if they are not represented by a member of the committee. Citizens have the ability to influence those elected officials who have a connection to the citizen. If you don't have a connection to the legislator—even though they may sit on a committee especially relevant to your cause—your job is to build or identify a connection. Only through some tangible political link can an interested party influence a congressional committee.

Chapter 6

Face-to-Face
Meetings

6.1 Tips for Meeting with Legislators or Staff

When in Washington, members of the U.S. House of Representatives will typically meet with five to eight groups of constituents each day—her combined staff could meet with another 20. Each group is petitioning the legislator or staffer with its cause: asking the legislator to cosponsor legislation, to vote "yea" or "nay" in an upcoming vote, or to request an earmark from the House or Senate Appropriations Committee. These sessions tend to last 10–20 minutes, involve two to 20 constituents, and as Chart 1, page 34, notes, they are the most influential tool in any advocate's toolkit. Here are 10 tips for maximizing the potential for success when meeting with a legislator in Washington or a state capital.

1. Know who you're talking to

It's important to conduct research on the legislators you plan to meet with. Does she have some connection to my issue, either through background or current committee assignments? What recent legislative or press activity has she engaged in? What did her father do for a living? Any of these answers could potentially open the door to her support.

2. Know your issue

A U.S. senator told me there are two types of people he meets with: people who come prepared to meetings and people who don't. "If they come prepared, I listen to them. If they don't, they listen to me. The first group has much more influence," she said. Some groups think their strength in numbers alone will carry the day, or that consistently contributing to the legislator's campaign is all that's required. But those influence factors can be defeated by a thoughtful constituent with command of the facts.

3. Refine your presentation

You might have 15 minutes with a legislator or staffer to make your pitch. Should you deliver one of the most important speeches you will ever give unrehearsed? Take 30 minutes the day before your meeting and practice your presentation. Place the best arguments first. Say it aloud, in front of the mirror, or a spouse, or your cat. Do everything to ensure that a weak presentation will not diminish your good ideas.

4. Don't arrive too early

Office space on Capitol Hill is cramped. It is amusing when *West Wing* episodes portrayed a White House staffer meeting on Capitol Hill in huge, mahogany-lined offices, with waiters serving coffee from silver pitchers. Because of the lack of space, offices literally cannot accommodate early arrivals. House offices may have one or two chairs—maybe a couch if they're lucky. Roam the halls, fix your hair, get some coffee, but don't arrive more than five minutes before the meeting.

5. Deliver your message in the first 10 minutes

Small talk and building rapport is important and necessary, but it's also important to get down to business quickly. Most constituent meetings with legislators in Washington last 15 minutes. Votes, important phone calls, and other distractions often interrupt meetings. After you've chatted about kids and sports, let her know why you're there.

6. Always have a specific "ask"

The most crucial role of advocacy in our democratic process is to hold elected officials accountable. But how can you hold them accountable if you don't have anything specific to hold them accountable to? Advocates should have specific requests—usually with a "yes/no" option—to create a metric that the legislator can be measured by. In 2005 Judge John Roberts was up for nomination to be Chief Justice of the Supreme Court. One national group launched an email campaign urging supporters to send messages asking senators to, "Ask tough questions of Judge Roberts." How do you hold a senator accountable to a request like that? Do you really think a senator was going to reply to that message with, "Actually, I favor the easy questions for Supreme Court nominees, like their favorite movie or baseball team."

7. Never go off-message

At the start of a meeting with a well-known business group and a senator, we expected the leader of the group to discuss the tax issue that had brought him and 10 other businessmen to Washington. Instead, he began the conversation by saying, "Our lobbyist wants us to tell you about (issue crucial to industry survival) . . . but instead I want to talk to you about abortion." Consistency in message between hired lobbyists and local advocates is essential to any successful advocacy efforts. The impulse to "freelance" usually ends in disaster. Interest groups, associations, and companies keep full time staff in Washington and state capitals for a reason—to identify those issues most relevant to the group and guide supporters with the correct message. Activists who don't follow their professional staff's advice may feel good about the liberating experience, but they're actually acting against their own interests.

8. The less paper, the better

Environmentalists would cry if they saw the amount of wasted reports, memos, and other hard-copy data that is disposed of daily on Capitol Hill. The average legislative assistant gets *three to four feet* of paper a week. Most of it is discarded without being read. Instead, staff will hold on to (and may even file) one- or two-page documents that succinctly summarize an issue. Emailing information is the best form of communication. As one chief of staff told me, "If you want to get your message to my boss, you better give it to me in a format I can cut and paste."

9. Provide feedback to professional lobbyists

One of the rare qualities that distinguish strong advocacy efforts from weak ones is close coordination between grassroots advocates and professional advocates. After meeting with a legislator or staff person it is *essential* that supporters provide feedback on the outcome of the meeting. If your group has an in-house lobbyist, she is going to file and track that data. When the legislator wavers, your professional advocate will politely remind him of his pledge to a constituent.

10. Follow-up within two weeks

When public officials are posed a specific question or request, they sometimes reply, "I'll look into it and get back to you." Either because of the crush of work or political necessity, sometimes they won't get back to you. The responsibility falls on the grassroots supporter to follow up. In most cases, the legislator or staffer has accidentally let the issue or question fall through the cracks, so a follow-up call is needed to prompt the elected official to make a decision. It also says to the official, "I'm not going away until you answer this question."

If you go in a group, determine before the meeting who's got the best story. As noted earlier, the personal story trumps all. A pro-life Republican congressman told me how he bucked his party and decided to support federal funding for stem cell research. He said a group of families who had children with juvenile diabetes came during a national group's advocacy day. One teenager talked about his life, how he coped with the disease, and his hope that the research could someday lead to a cure. "It was just one of those meetings that had a huge impact," the congressman said.

Finally, appreciate that a legislator may often be in a tough spot. Most constituents, even some lobbyists, fail to understand that a lawmaker may genuinely want to please two groups of constituents who are pitted against one another. The wise citizen-petitioner will empathize with the struggling politician, perhaps even gaining his trust. "I particularly admire someone who's able to articulate the opposing argument, that can give a good faith account of the other side," said one House Democrat. "They seem to understand my situation, and I respect that."

6.2 How to Influence Legislators at Town Hall Meetings

Town hall meetings are excellent opportunities to get a legislator to make a public commitment or to meet with him privately after the meeting. In addition to using the forums to espouse or defend their positions, many legislators use town hall meetings as a source for their own legislative agenda. "The best ideas I get for legislation come from town hall meetings," said one House Democratic subcommittee chairman. These meetings are usually announced to constituents through mailed postcards or emails.

Members of Congress are incredibly attentive to constituents who attend town hall meetings. One House Republican said he uses them like focus groups. "I'll offer up three to five issues," he said. "You get more off-the-cuff, unrehearsed reaction to issues. A town hall meeting is one way of getting off-the-street consensus." During August 2009, thousands of citizens attended congressional town hall meetings to voice an opinion on President Barack Obama's health care proposal. Some (not many) looked like raucous shout matches. These are extremely rare. Most congressional town hall meetings are attended by 20–40 constituents, who politely ask their congressman questions or offer opinions.

Here are the top 10 strategies for taking advantage of these unique opportunities:

1. Be prepared

Most people don't approach their member of Congress with a well-researched, well-rehearsed pitch. Constituents who come to town hall meetings with thoughtful arguments, good data, and persuasive stories get remembered.

2. Tell a personal story

As noted in § 5.2, page 38, members of Congress are always looking for firsthand accounts of the impact that policies have on their constituents. Think in advance about how a policy might affect you or your family, business, or community.

3. Use numbers if you have them

As shown in Chart 1, page 34, someone representing other constituents, such as a union leader, company owner, or association president, is extremely influential to lawmakers. Use numbers by mentioning things like, "I have 50 employees," "I represent 100 people in my union," or "There are 500 people in my community affected by this bill."

4. Be polite

Some constituents start a conversation with, "I pay your salary so you better listen to me." During August 2009, tens of thousands of Americans attended congressional town hall meetings—some people used the forums to shout at their legislator. It doesn't matter if you're talking to your grocer or a public official—starting any conversation with another person in a rude manner is not a very tactful way to persuade them. As one House Democrat said, "I appreciate a heartfelt expression of conviction and willingness to discuss as well as assert. I respect those who reason and are willing to have a dialogue instead of just shouting and pounding on the table."

5. Go in groups

Nothing says "listen to me" to a public official like a crowd. This is not to suggest that you should bring pitch forks and torches to your next town hall meeting, but a polite chorus is better than a solo performance.

6. Talk to staff

Every legislator brings staff to town hall meetings. Tell them your story before the meeting (also ask a public question during the meeting) and get their business cards. You'll be creating a champion for your cause within the office. (Also see § 6.4, page 53.)

7. Leave paper

Any documents passed to state-based staff will likely be faxed to the legislative assistant in Washington who covers your issue. One senator takes the documents he collects at his town hall meetings and personally delivers them to legislative assistants in his Washington office. Where do you think those requests for help rank on his assistant's to-do list?

8. Follow up politely

Politely persistent people persuade politicians. Congressional offices are often overworked, so an elected official often responds to an individual who follows up with a reminder phone call a few weeks after attending a meeting.

9. Get your people to multiple meetings

When a member hears the same obscure question in a large town that he hears in a small town, the member of Congress will wonder, "Why is *everyone* asking about this?" Hearing the same thing in different places signals to a politician that there may be a deeper problem afoot.

10. Provide feedback to professional lobbyists

After interacting with a lawmaker in the district, it is vital that constituents who are part of groups provide feedback on what happened in that interaction to their Washington government relations office. Some groups provide feedback forms online, others make their email addresses available to members/supporters. Even providing the feedback to a local contact, such as a state association, will ensure an "accountability loop" is closed. The next time your professional lobbyist meets with a legislator he'll mention your town hall meeting question—and the public official will know that he can't say one thing back home and another thing in Washington.

6.3 How to Turn a Chance Meeting into a Legislative Victory

So you're in the supermarket, waiting in line, and who's behind you but your member of Congress. Should you press her with your favorite issue and intrude on what is clearly her "personal time"? The answer is, "YES!" Legislators expect that as public figures they will be subject to all degrees of influence when they are in public. A polite and respectful request is not only expected, but often welcome, as legislators use these encounters as yet another barometer of public opinion.

For example, one member of Congress was coaching first base for his son's Little League team when a mother on the opposing team took the opportunity to lecture him on the correct U.S. policy for the Middle East. "That kind of citizen interaction rolls in your head every day and it forms a basis of knowledge that I can act upon," he said. If you've got an opportunity for a one-on-one, grab it—then herald the interaction on your organization's blog or web site. One Democratic senator said it this way: "When I'm at home and I've had individual citizens come tell me about a problem, and then I continue to hear about it, I do something about it. It's the repetitiveness of it. I go home and get the temperature of things. So I say to people, don't hesitate to mention something to an elected official."

6.4 Influencing Staff, and Why It's Important

For folks visiting Washington to meet with their congressional office, you might be surprised that you don't get to meet with the congresswoman herself or her chief of staff, and instead meet with an aide— usually a very young person who doesn't look old enough to buy a drink, much less understand your issue. "People assume that if they jump right to the chief of staff, they'll get answers," said one Republican House chief of staff. "They are wasting their time."

The reality is that young person is the best and brightest America has to offer. Capitol Hill is one of the most competitive work environments in America. Hundreds of resumes come in for every job posted. Those selected to serve often come from the best schools in the nation or in the legislator's home state, and have stellar academic records and multiple internships on their resumes. When they arrive in DC they get handed a portfolio of complex issues they must master, regularly work 12-hour days, and get paid about 1/3 less than they would make in the private sector.

Congressional staff are the silent patriots who keep the system running. In Washington they are overwhelmingly young, single, and idealistic. The *average* work week is about 60 hours, and Saturday or evening duty is pretty standard (usually to catch up on answering constituent mail or to attend a local function in the state). If you spend some time around these people you'll discover that there are some Americans who still respond to John F. Kennedy's appeal, "Ask what you can do for your country."

When meeting with a "staffer," build rapport in the same way you would with a legislator. Probe to determine how much the assistant genuinely knows about your issue, and offer to educate him. Most of the time a smart legislative assistant (known as "LA") will not make a commitment to the request or question posed, unless the legislator already has decided the issue. But if you have a specific request the staffer will invariably take it to the legislator for a response.

It's always a good idea to get a business card from the staffer. Follow up in a day or two with a thank-you email. Then, follow up again in two weeks to see if the legislator has made a decision on the issue. And, if you think that this cherubic public servant isn't worth your time, just remember: this wunderkind is the legislator's chief advisor on the issue most important to you, and may be the last person he speaks with before making a final decision on your request.

Chapter 7
Communications

The most common methods for citizens to interact with elected officials are through emails, letters, faxes, or phone calls. The cynical view is that with the growth of the Internet and increased communications to Capitol Hill, the value of these communications has diminished. However, constituent communications are more important than ever. "The most important thing that people should understand is that mail matters more than most constituents think it does," said one Republican senator. "There might be 100 different answers from a 100 different senators, but each one will tell the same basic thing: that mail has more of an impact than any citizen realizes," he said.

A good old-fashioned letter is still a valuable way to communicate to legislators. Like email and faxes, letters are sorted daily by staff and interns into categories, date stamped, and logged into office software called a "Correspondence Management System." In October 2001, two members of Congress and several news organizations were sent letters containing the deadly toxin anthrax, killing five people. As a result, all postal communications sent to legislators' Washington offices are now irradiated to kill any toxic substance included with the letter. This process delays all letters and postcards sent to Congress by one to three weeks.

Email is the most effective way to send a written communication to legislators. As congressional offices enhance their technology, email is often quickly integrated into tracking systems, instantly notifying legislators of constituents' opinions. The most sophisticated software can even measure how much of the email message was a template text and drafted by a group organizing a campaign and how much was written by the sender. Given the speed of delivery, ability of offices to quickly assess the writer's opinion and respond to it, and flexibility to include links to other valuable persuasive components (such as video or links to more information), email remains one of the most versatile and effective tool for advocates.

One of the least effective tools is the fax. Fax campaigns are *hated* by congressional offices because of the administrative burden created by this 1970s technology. Similarly, postcard campaigns, the staple of advocacy communications in the 1980s and 1990s, are also spurned on Capitol Hill as the data cannot be easily integrated into computer systems without costly manual data entry.

7.1 How to Write Letters and Emails to Legislators that Influence Decision-Making

What always distinguishes good communications from weak ones isn't the vehicle by which they arrive, but the writing. As noted in Chart 1, page 34, next to having a one-on-one meeting with your congressman, sending an email or letter is the most effective way to influence undecided lawmakers. It is remarkable how easy it is to write an influential email to Congress, and how few people write good ones. Much of the communications that flow into congressional offices are angry rants, which is why when someone sends in a well-written argument, the note will often be put in a legislator's "to read" file. Below is the construction of a model communication to a legislator.

● Paragraph 1—Establish your standing

The emails and letters most likely to influence legislators are those from individuals who are personally affected by a policy, or have some knowledge of the impact. You see parents of children with diseases who start the letters with, "My child has juvenile diabetes and I think we should increase research funding." It's a likely bet that the congressman is going to see that letter and respond quickly. It also helps to note that you're a voter. (If you are not a registered voter, please put down this book immediately and go register to vote. You cannot be a truly effective advocate without voting.)

● Paragraph 2—Communicate a personal story

Why should this legislator listen to you (other than the fact the Constitution requires him to)? The *power* that advocates possesses primarily rests in their personal story. Tell a story in a compelling way, communicating both emotion and fact. (For more on the value of a personal story, see § 5.2, page 38.)

• Paragraph 3— Include a specific "ask"

As with every interaction with an elected official, be specific in what you request. "Please cosponsor this bill." "Please go to the House floor and speak on behalf of this project." A letter to a congressman from an earlier era had a specific ask while demonstrating the constituent's support. It read: "Dear Congressman. I voted for you three times and I think you are wonderful. Please send me $900 at once so I can buy an icebox and repaint my car. Sincerely, John. PS. The three times I voted for you were in the election of 1946."

• Paragraph 4—Include local data

Lawmakers crave accurate information on the impact of proposed policies or laws on their constituency. With hundreds of issues pending before Congress, legislators need reliable data on how their decisions might affect constituents. This doesn't mean you need to do a vast research project—do a quick survey of 10 or 20 people who share the same interests and provide those findings to the legislator.

• Paragraph 5—Communicate passion

If you don't have a vested interest in a policy question you can still communicate how strongly you feel about it. Threats are not effective, but enthusiasm is. The occasional underlined sentence or exclamation point tells the legislator that crossing this voter may result in a newly minted volunteer for his opponent's campaign. Conversely, writing in all CAPS and in the paper margins is the equivalent of shouting and is not effective.

One Republican congressman summed it up this way: "What I look for in communications is not just 'I'm for' or 'I'm against' something, I look for why you are for or against something."

7.2 What Kind of Mail Do Lawmakers Really Read?

There is an extraordinary cynicism in America about the degree to which legislators listen to their constituents. This is partly manifested through the tacit belief that messages sent to legislators are not really integrated into policy decision-making. And, most people believe that if the messages are read, they're only read by staff or interns. This belief is mostly inaccurate.

Nearly all constituent communications are counted and responded to by members of Congress and staff. And legislators spend hours each week reading and responding to constituent correspondence. (See Chart 1, page 34, for details.) Individualized communications with some expression of personal sentiment or opinion are most likely to be influential. The importance of constituent mail was best expressed by a Senate chief of staff who participated in a focus group conducted in November 2001, two months after the 9/11 terrorist attacks on New York and Washington, and one month after an anthrax attack had completely shut down the delivery of paper mail to the U.S. Congress. He noted that his boss (the senator) felt cut off. "He feels like he doesn't know what's going on," the chief of staff said. "He really misses the mail."

Nearly all legislators use constituent communications as a gauge of public opinion. But not all letters, emails, or faxes reach the desk of a member of Congress. While all communications are usually aggregated into the "for" or "against" category, some stand out. Staff identify communications that in some way help the legislator understand constituents' feelings. Or, perhaps the communication validates or contests the legislator's opinion. Or, sometimes they just make her feel good.

Below are the types and characteristics of communications most likely to be sifted by staff and presented to legislators as representative of public opinion.

• Well-Written

A carefully crafted message still carries weight. The value and power of the written word has not changed since the times of Homer.

• Passionate

Those who can convey feeling in a message are most likely to be read by those who must make decisions. Everyone wishes to be moved by words, even members of Congress.

• Funny

Think about the email you forward to friends. Then think about how you can convey that feeling in a communication to a legislator, while still making your point.

• Written by Children

The younger generation holds a special place in the policy process. Communications from kids get special attention in nearly every legislator's office, as public officials feel it is part of their responsibility to teach the next generation about the role of government and democracy in society.

• Insightful

Some communications present ideas or data not previously offered to the legislator. If a staff member catches this, she is very likely to present it to her boss.

• Representative of a Group

Staff will sometimes identify communications that may not be well written or passionate, but that convey a view that articulates the opinion of many in the district. Staff are looking for both quantitative and qualitative data to help legislators make decisions, and sometimes an email that just articulates the "average Joe's" opinion is helpful in understanding the opinions of thousands of "average Joes."

• Thank You Notes

A guaranteed way of seeing that your email gets printed and put on the desk of a member of Congress is to say "thank you." Very few groups or individuals thank legislators for the work they do, so those few who do get their messages passed on to the boss. It's not just a polite thing to do—it likely will be remembered the next time the legislator is visited by the citizen or the professional lobbyist who represents them.

Finally, recognize one doesn't need to be loud to be heard. Members and staff regularly share stories of the worst nasty-grams sent by constituents. The thoughtful message will always triumph over a hateful one. One constituent of a Colorado congresswoman actually deposited, along with her note, a small pile of doggy do-do at the congressional office. The office had her prosecuted for "criminal use of a noxious substance," but she was acquitted. The jury ruled that delivering canine excrement to Congress is free speech under the First Amendment. Nevertheless, remember that the most effective message is usually not the most noxious one.

7.3 How One Letter Reached the Oval Office and Fed a Million People

In 2004 President George W. Bush was in the White House Rose Garden signing a bill related to hunger. Among those attending this signing ceremony was Senator Richard Lugar, chairman of the Senate Foreign Relations Committee, and David Beckmann, president of Bread for the World, a church-based nonprofit that seeks to reduce hunger and fight AIDS worldwide.

Dr. Beckmann saw an opportunity to give a pitch to the leader of the free world for another program close to his organization's heart, the Millennium Challenge Account, which seeks to relieve hunger in the eight poorest nations in the world. It had received $1 billion in funding in 2004, but like any good advocate, David Beckmann wanted more.

He approached the President and asked him to increase funding for the Millennium Challenge Account, pointing out how much good just a little additional funding could do. President Bush asked his friend, the chairman of the Senate Foreign Relations Committee, Senator Lugar, what he thought of this program. Senator Lugar said, "You know, I am just now responding to a letter from a constituent, Mrs. Connie Wick of Indianapolis. She is saying just what you are saying, David, that we should fully fund the Millennium Account, the AIDS initiative, and not cut funding for ongoing programs to help poor people."

At the time, Connie Wick was 83 years old and lived in Robin Run Retirement Community on Happy Hollow Road in Indianapolis, Ind. She was not a wealthy contributor to a political party, had never run for public office, did not lead legions of followers, and never went golfing with a member of Congress. She was one voice, one person, who felt that America should do more to help feed the hungry. In the President's proposed budget for the following year, the Millennium Account funding rose from $1 billion a year to $2.5 billion.

Perhaps it's just a coincidence. Or perhaps the President of the United States, when he was considering the budget for the next year, had Connie Wick's words in mind. As you consider your role in the democratic process, remember that you have the power to change the world. And, remember the most important lesson our founding fathers taught us: Politics is too important to be left to politicians.

7.4 Effective (and Ineffective) Phone Calls to Legislators

Nearly every legislator reviews phone tallies when hot issues are before a legislature. Assistants are charged with recording the number of constituents who call pro and con on an issue, providing the lawmaker with an instant poll on a topic. It's far from scientific, but still has value to a politician. Phone calls provide more *qualitative* data than written correspondence to legislators, as staff can gauge the emotion in a callers voice. Many members of Congress, after observing a harried staff assistant taking dozens of calls on an issue, will ask the young aide at the end of the day, "How mad are they?" For the U.S. Congress, it's best to call the Washington office. Nearly all congressional offices base their constituent correspondence/communications operation in Washington, so your call is most likely to be quickly logged with the right people. Keep the call short, one to three minutes. Long calls from constituents suggest a "wacky" factor and might result in your message being ignored.

Some groups also set up or hire phone banks to generate calls to lawmakers' offices. This can be effective *only if* the callers are trained on how to make the call. Congressional staff can spot canned, unmotivated callers in a split second. In contrast, when the callers who are identified have clear interests, are provided the right talking points to help them, and are connected to offices over a short period of time (a couple of days), the impact can be powerful. A few do's and don't's:

* **Do** note that you are a constituent early in the conversation. That triggers a response on the other end of the phone, "Oh, this call is important."

* **Do** reference a specific bill or decision that is pending with the legislator. Vague references will be ignored.

* **Do** give an email address (preferred) or street address and ask for a reply. This verifies you are a constituent and ensures a degree of accountability.

* **Do** be polite. The Constitution gives you the right to raise the issue, but not to yell at a staff assistant.

* **Don't** pretend to be some important muckety-muck if you're not. The line "I once went skeet shooting with the congressman's third cousin" isn't really the ticket to greater influence.

- **Don't** threaten with your vote, campaign contribution or anything of value if the legislator doesn't do what you want. Legislators get paid to listen to you and they are excellent assessors of calculating the consequences of crossing constituents.

7.5 Why Online Petitions Usually Fail to Influence Congress

There are groups that lobby Congress who love petitions. Many web sites have popped up offering visitors the chance to create their own petition and send it to Congress. Regrettably, some of these sites are simply "data mining" operations. They convince you to give them your email address and identify some issue that interests you, and then sell the data to a group that will seek your donation or support.

Few congressional offices read or acknowledge petitions unless they are hand-signed, with constituent addresses included, and demonstrate a strong opinion (with big numbers) on an issue relevant to the office. The best, and virtually only way to use petitions in an advocacy campaign is as a prop. Get a few thousand folks to pen their name and address on a statement, then ship the rumpled, stained, and loosely wrapped package to your professional advocate in Washington. She'll use it the next time she has a meeting with a legislator to demonstrate support or opposition back home to an issue.

7.6 How to Write Letters to the Editor that Get Published

Letters to the editor are used for a variety of purposes in public debate. They are used to respond to criticism, correct an inaccuracy, complain about the slant of coverage, point out a missing fact in a story, or amplify an element of the story in an interesting way. In the advocacy world, letters to the editor are an excellent complement to directly contacting legislators and by raising public awareness. They are also one of the best ways to get a legislator's attention.

As a congressional press secretary I could hand my boss a stack of clips from the front page of every newspaper in the district that said he walked on water. And yet he could quickly scan the reef of papers and find one line in a letter to the editor of a weekly paper with a circulation smaller than a church bulletin, and say to me: "Did you see what this guy said about me on page 37 in paragraph 4 opposite the ad for the furniture auction?" Legislators are creatures with egos, and they want to be loved by everyone. One or two lines of criticism (or praise) might seem meaningless in a broad effort to sway opinion, but if you mention the name of a member of Congress in a letter to the editor it will be read by the person you most want to influence.

Here are the rules for writing letters to the editor that will get published.

First, editors are more likely to run your letter if it references a story that ran in the paper during the last week. In fact, it's almost impossible to get a letter to the editor published that does not reference a story. If possible, include it in the first sentence of the letter.

Second, keep the letters short—100 to 200 words, or two to four paragraphs. Succinct, strong, and powerful language is much more likely to gain an editor's attention than long-winded rants, or even thoughtful, but lengthy, arguments. Like a lawmaker, editors are much more attracted to stories from someone who has an *interest* or *connection* to an issue, rather than those just expressing an opinion. Those with a personal story to tell about an issue have an advantage over those that do not. Also, anyone who is representative of a group warrants attention. Even those who chair a small neighborhood committee are perceived to speak for others and are therefore good candidates for publication.

If you see appropriate language on a web site of an organization you support, use it as a foundation for your writing, but do not send it to the newspaper verbatim. Some grassroots organizations and political campaigns are smart about organizing letter-to-the-editor campaigns, and they are a valuable and ethical component of any advocacy effort. However, if an editor sees two letters with identical copy, he will consider the letter "manufactured" and will not run it. Use your own words to express your feelings.

Third, a reference to the legislator is a must. If the lawmaker has ignored you or your issue, letters to the editor are a great way to get his attention. In contrast, if the lawmaker has supported your issue, *definitely* write a letter to the editor. It's also very wise to send a copy to the legislator's office (directed to his chief aide). Even if the letter isn't published, you will be sending a potent message that you have the power (and inclination) to influence thousands of voters. The voice of one person in the letters to the editor section can confer as much credibility than a roomful of politicians.

Finally, if appropriate, tell allies how they can get involved. Some newspapers refuse to run web site addresses (this is perhaps a fleeting attempt to block the Internet from putting them out of existence). Include organization names or relevant clubs—anything that points a potential recruit in the right direction.

7.7 Thank or Spank: After-the-Vote Communications

After the issue has been decided and voted on, is there any value in communicating with legislators to either praise them (thank), or condemn them (spank)? The answer is a resounding "Yes!"

Thank you notes to legislators are a rarity. Anytime one is sent to a member of Congress it is immediately put at the top of his "to be read" pile. It might even be read aloud at the next staff meeting. Then, the next time you or your group has an issue before that legislator, he and his staff are going to start the discussion with that fond memory in mind.

Conversely, it is important for you to communicate your disappointment with legislators who do not support you. This should be done politely and professionally, but firmly. Don't include threats such as, "I'm not going to vote for you now." It comes across to the legislator and staff as petulant. Instead, express the wish that the *next time* the issue comes up, you hope he will reconsider his position. Or, perhaps you have another issue that could arise in the future where you would find mutual agreement. The value here is to make sure the legislator knows that he is accountable—and that you're watching. It has a psychological impact on public officials and forces them to be ever mindful of those individuals and groups who persistently and politely never let them out of their sight.

7.8 The Magic of Combining Advocacy Tactics

At the beginning of the 20th century neurophysiologist Dr. Charles Sherrington was curious about dogs. He wanted to know why, when you rubbed a dog's belly, he would invariably shake his back leg. Dr. Sherrington discovered that you could produce the same result if you slightly rubbed the dog's belly while simultaneously patting his head.

Well, politicians are a little like dogs. They respond to intense pressure of one kind, or they respond to moderate pressure from a multitude of sources. When legislators are confronted with a difficult decision they bring together senior staff to get input. The legislative director says, "We've gotten 500 letters in favor of this bill." The district director says, "I've heard two community association presidents would support it." The press secretary says, "There have been three letters to the editor endorsing it." And the chief of staff says, "And I've gotten two calls from leadership asking you to vote 'yes'." At that point, there's no further debate—the member will say, "OK, let's do it ... What's next?" (Credit to Dr. Alan Rosenblatt, the discoveror of this connection between "Sherrington's Law" and online advocacy.)

Appendices

Appendix A
The U.S. Constitution and Amendments

Appendix B
The Declaration of Independence

Appendix C
The Advocate's Pledge

Appendix D
How to Analyze a Legislator's Perception of Our Issue

Appendix E
How Legislators Perceive Issues

Appendix F
Information about Congress and Washington, DC

Appendix G
Legislative Process Flowchart

Appendix H
State and Local Resources

Appendix A
The Constitution of the United States

We the People of the United States, in Order to form a more perfect Union, establish Justice, insure domestic Tranquility, provide for the common defence, promote the general Welfare, and secure the Blessings of Liberty to ourselves and our Posterity, do ordain and establish this Constitution for the United States of America.

Article. I.

Section. 1.

All legislative Powers herein granted shall be vested in a Congress of the United States, which shall consist of a Senate and House of Representatives.

Section. 2.

The House of Representatives shall be composed of Members chosen every second Year by the People of the several States, and the Electors in each State shall have the Qualifications requisite for Electors of the most numerous Branch of the State Legislature.

No Person shall be a Representative who shall not have attained to the Age of twenty five Years, and been seven Years a Citizen of the United States, and who shall not, when elected, be an Inhabitant of that State in which he shall be chosen.

Representatives and direct Taxes shall be apportioned among the several States which may be included within this Union, according to their respective Numbers, which shall be determined by adding to the whole Number of free Persons, including those bound to Service for a Term of Years, and excluding Indians not taxed, three fifths of all other Persons. The actual Enumeration shall be made within three Years after the first Meeting of the Congress of the United States, and within every subsequent Term of ten Years, in such Manner as they shall by Law direct. The Number of Representatives shall not exceed one for every thirty Thousand, but each State shall have at Least one Representative; and until such enumeration shall be made, the State of New Hampshire

For a free Pocket Constitution, see <www.TCNPocket.com>.

shall be entitled to chuse three, Massachusetts eight, Rhode-Island and Providence Plantations one, Connecticut five, New-York six, New Jersey four, Pennsylvania eight, Delaware one, Maryland six, Virginia ten, North Carolina five, South Carolina five, and Georgia three.

When vacancies happen in the Representation from any State, the Executive Authority thereof shall issue Writs of Election to fill such Vacancies.

The House of Representatives shall chuse their Speaker and other Officers; and shall have the sole Power of Impeachment.

Section. 3.

The Senate of the United States shall be composed of two Senators from each State, chosen by the Legislature thereof for six Years; and each Senator shall have one Vote.

Immediately after they shall be assembled in Consequence of the first Election, they shall be divided as equally as may be into three Classes. The Seats of the Senators of the first Class shall be vacated at the Expiration of the second Year, of the second Class at the Expiration of the fourth Year, and of the third Class at the Expiration of the sixth Year, so that one third may be chosen every second Year; and if Vacancies happen by Resignation, or otherwise, during the Recess of the Legislature of any State, the Executive thereof may make temporary Appointments until the next Meeting of the Legislature, which shall then fill such Vacancies.

No Person shall be a Senator who shall not have attained to the Age of thirty Years, and been nine Years a Citizen of the United States, and who shall not, when elected, be an Inhabitant of that State for which he shall be chosen.

The Vice President of the United States shall be President of the Senate, but shall have no Vote, unless they be equally divided.

The Senate shall chuse their other Officers, and also a President pro tempore, in the Absence of the Vice President, or when he shall exercise the Office of President of the United States.

The Senate shall have the sole Power to try all Impeachments. When sitting for that Purpose, they shall be on Oath or Affirmation. When the President of the United States is tried, the Chief Justice shall preside: And no Person shall be convicted without the Concurrence of two thirds of the Members present.

For a free Pocket Constitution, see <www.TCNPocket.com>.

Judgment in Cases of Impeachment shall not extend further than to removal from Office, and disqualification to hold and enjoy any Office of honor, Trust or Profit under the United States: but the Party convicted shall nevertheless be liable and subject to Indictment, Trial, Judgment and Punishment, according to Law.

Section. 4.

The Times, Places and Manner of holding Elections for Senators and Representatives, shall be prescribed in each State by the Legislature thereof; but the Congress may at any time by Law make or alter such Regulations, except as to the Places of chusing Senators.

The Congress shall assemble at least once in every Year, and such Meeting shall be on the first Monday in December, unless they shall by Law appoint a different Day.

Section. 5.

Each House shall be the Judge of the Elections, Returns and Qualifications of its own Members, and a Majority of each shall constitute a Quorum to do Business; but a smaller Number may adjourn from day to day, and may be authorized to compel the Attendance of absent Members, in such Manner, and under such Penalties as each House may provide.

Each House may determine the Rules of its Proceedings, punish its Members for disorderly Behaviour, and, with the Concurrence of two thirds, expel a Member.

Each House shall keep a Journal of its Proceedings, and from time to time publish the same, excepting such Parts as may in their Judgment require Secrecy; and the Yeas and Nays of the Members of either House on any question shall, at the Desire of one fifth of those Present, be entered on the Journal.

Neither House, during the Session of Congress, shall, without the Consent of the other, adjourn for more than three days, nor to any other Place than that in which the two Houses shall be sitting.

Section. 6.

The Senators and Representatives shall receive a Compensation for their Services, to be ascertained by Law, and paid out of the Treasury of the United States. They shall in all Cases, except Treason, Felony and Breach of the Peace, be privileged from Arrest during their Atten-

For a free Pocket Constitution, see <www.TCNPocket.com>.

dance at the Session of their respective Houses, and in going to and returning from the same; and for any Speech or Debate in either House, they shall not be questioned in any other Place.

No Senator or Representative shall, during the Time for which he was elected, be appointed to any civil Office under the Authority of the United States, which shall have been created, or the Emoluments whereof shall have been encreased during such time; and no Person holding any Office under the United States, shall be a Member of either House during his Continuance in Office.

Section. 7.

All Bills for raising Revenue shall originate in the House of Representatives; but the Senate may propose or concur with Amendments as on other Bills.

Every Bill which shall have passed the House of Representatives and the Senate, shall, before it become a Law, be presented to the President of the United States: If he approve he shall sign it, but if not he shall return it, with his Objections to that House in which it shall have originated, who shall enter the Objections at large on their Journal, and proceed to reconsider it. If after such Reconsideration two thirds of that House shall agree to pass the Bill, it shall be sent, together with the Objections, to the other House, by which it shall likewise be reconsidered, and if approved by two thirds of that House, it shall become a Law. But in all such Cases the Votes of both Houses shall be determined by yeas and Nays, and the Names of the Persons voting for and against the Bill shall be entered on the Journal of each House respectively. If any Bill shall not be returned by the President within ten Days (Sundays excepted) after it shall have been presented to him, the Same shall be a Law, in like Manner as if he had signed it, unless the Congress by their Adjournment prevent its Return, in which Case it shall not be a Law.

Every Order, Resolution, or Vote to which the Concurrence of the Senate and House of Representatives may be necessary (except on a question of Adjournment) shall be presented to the President of the United States; and before the Same shall take Effect, shall be approved by him, or being disapproved by him, shall be repassed by two thirds of the Senate and House of Representatives, according to the Rules and Limitations prescribed in the Case of a Bill.

For a free Pocket Constitution, see <www.TCNPocket.com>.

Section. 8.

The Congress shall have Power To lay and collect Taxes, Duties, Imposts and Excises, to pay the Debts and provide for the common Defence and general Welfare of the United States; but all Duties, Imposts and Excises shall be uniform throughout the United States;

To borrow Money on the credit of the United States;

To regulate Commerce with foreign Nations, and among the several States, and with the Indian Tribes;

To establish an uniform Rule of Naturalization, and uniform Laws on the subject of Bankruptcies throughout the United States;

To coin Money, regulate the Value thereof, and of foreign Coin, and fix the Standard of Weights and Measures;

To provide for the Punishment of counterfeiting the Securities and current Coin of the United States;

To establish Post Offices and post Roads;

To promote the Progress of Science and useful Arts, by securing for limited Times to Authors and Inventors the exclusive Right to their respective Writings and Discoveries;

To constitute Tribunals inferior to the supreme Court;

To define and punish Piracies and Felonies committed on the high Seas, and Offences against the Law of Nations;

To declare War, grant Letters of Marque and Reprisal, and make Rules concerning Captures on Land and Water;

To raise and support Armies, but no Appropriation of Money to that Use shall be for a longer Term than two Years;

To provide and maintain a Navy;

To make Rules for the Government and Regulation of the land and naval Forces;

To provide for calling forth the Militia to execute the Laws of the Union, suppress Insurrections and repel Invasions;

To provide for organizing, arming, and disciplining, the Militia, and for governing such Part of them as may be employed in the Service

For a free Pocket Constitution, see <www.TCNPocket.com>.

of the United States, reserving to the States respectively, the Appointment of the Officers, and the Authority of training the Militia according to the discipline prescribed by Congress;

To exercise exclusive Legislation in all Cases whatsoever, over such District (not exceeding ten Miles square) as may, by Cession of particular States, and the Acceptance of Congress, become the Seat of the Government of the United States, and to exercise like Authority over all Places purchased by the Consent of the Legislature of the State in which the Same shall be, for the Erection of Forts, Magazines, Arsenals, dock-Yards, and other needful Buildings;—And

To make all Laws which shall be necessary and proper for carrying into Execution the foregoing Powers, and all other Powers vested by this Constitution in the Government of the United States, or in any Department or Officer thereof.

Section. 9.

The Migration or Importation of such Persons as any of the States now existing shall think proper to admit, shall not be prohibited by the Congress prior to the Year one thousand eight hundred and eight, but a Tax or duty may be imposed on such Importation, not exceeding ten dollars for each Person.

The Privilege of the Writ of Habeas Corpus shall not be suspended, unless when in Cases of Rebellion or Invasion the public Safety may require it.

No Bill of Attainder or ex post facto Law shall be passed.

No Capitation, or other direct, Tax shall be laid, unless in Proportion to the Census or enumeration herein before directed to be taken.

No Tax or Duty shall be laid on Articles exported from any State.

No Preference shall be given by any Regulation of Commerce or Revenue to the Ports of one State over those of another; nor shall Vessels bound to, or from, one State, be obliged to enter, clear, or pay Duties in another.

No Money shall be drawn from the Treasury, but in Consequence of Appropriations made by Law; and a regular Statement and Account of the Receipts and Expenditures of all public Money shall be published from time to time.

No Title of Nobility shall be granted by the United States: And no

Person holding any Office of Profit or Trust under them, shall, without the Consent of the Congress, accept of any present, Emolument, Office, or Title, of any kind whatever, from any King, Prince, or foreign State.

Section. 10.

No State shall enter into any Treaty, Alliance, or Confederation; grant Letters of Marque and Reprisal; coin Money; emit Bills of Credit; make any Thing but gold and silver Coin a Tender in Payment of Debts; pass any Bill of Attainder, ex post facto Law, or Law impairing the Obligation of Contracts, or grant any Title of Nobility.

No State shall, without the Consent of the Congress, lay any Imposts or Duties on Imports or Exports, except what may be absolutely necessary for executing it's inspection Laws: and the net Produce of all Duties and Imposts, laid by any State on Imports or Exports, shall be for the Use of the Treasury of the United States; and all such Laws shall be subject to the Revision and Controul of the Congress.

No State shall, without the Consent of Congress, lay any Duty of Tonnage, keep Troops, or Ships of War in time of Peace, enter into any Agreement or Compact with another State, or with a foreign Power, or engage in War, unless actually invaded, or in such imminent Danger as will not admit of delay.

Article. II.

Section. 1.

The executive Power shall be vested in a President of the United States of America. He shall hold his Office during the Term of four Years, and, together with the Vice President, chosen for the same Term, be elected, as follows:

Each State shall appoint, in such Manner as the Legislature thereof may direct, a Number of Electors, equal to the whole Number of Senators and Representatives to which the State may be entitled in the Congress: but no Senator or Representative, or Person holding an Office of Trust or Profit under the United States, shall be appointed an Elector.

The Electors shall meet in their respective States, and vote by Ballot for two Persons, of whom one at least shall not be an Inhabitant of the same State with themselves. And they shall make a List of all the

For a free Pocket Constitution, see <www.TCNPocket.com>.

Persons voted for, and of the Number of Votes for each; which List they shall sign and certify, and transmit sealed to the Seat of the Government of the United States, directed to the President of the Senate. The President of the Senate shall, in the Presence of the Senate and House of Representatives, open all the Certificates, and the Votes shall then be counted. The Person having the greatest Number of Votes shall be the President, if such Number be a Majority of the whole Number of Electors appointed; and if there be more than one who have such Majority, and have an equal Number of Votes, then the House of Representatives shall immediately chuse by Ballot one of them for President; and if no Person have a Majority, then from the five highest on the List the said House shall in like Manner chuse the President. But in chusing the President, the Votes shall be taken by States, the Representation from each State having one Vote; A quorum for this purpose shall consist of a Member or Members from two thirds of the States, and a Majority of all the States shall be necessary to a Choice. In every Case, after the Choice of the President, the Person having the greatest Number of Votes of the Electors shall be the Vice President. But if there should remain two or more who have equal Votes, the Senate shall chuse from them by Ballot the Vice President.

The Congress may determine the Time of chusing the Electors, and the Day on which they shall give their Votes; which Day shall be the same throughout the United States.

No Person except a natural born Citizen, or a Citizen of the United States, at the time of the Adoption of this Constitution, shall be eligible to the Office of President; neither shall any Person be eligible to that Office who shall not have attained to the Age of thirty five Years, and been fourteen Years a Resident within the United States.

In Case of the Removal of the President from Office, or of his Death, Resignation, or Inability to discharge the Powers and Duties of the said Office, the Same shall devolve on the Vice President, and the Congress may by Law provide for the Case of Removal, Death, Resignation or Inability, both of the President and Vice President, declaring what Officer shall then act as President, and such Officer shall act accordingly, until the Disability be removed, or a President shall be elected.

The President shall, at stated Times, receive for his Services, a Compensation, which shall neither be increased nor diminished during the Period for which he shall have been elected, and he shall not receive

For a free Pocket Constitution, see <www.TCNPocket.com>.

within that Period any other Emolument from the United States, or any of them.

Before he enter on the Execution of his Office, he shall take the following Oath or Affirmation:—"I do solemnly swear (or affirm) that I will faithfully execute the Office of President of the United States, and will to the best of my Ability, preserve, protect and defend the Constitution of the United States."

Section. 2.

The President shall be Commander in Chief of the Army and Navy of the United States, and of the Militia of the several States, when called into the actual Service of the United States; he may require the Opinion, in writing, of the principal Officer in each of the executive Departments, upon any Subject relating to the Duties of their respective Offices, and he shall have Power to grant Reprieves and Pardons for Offences against the United States, except in Cases of Impeachment.

He shall have Power, by and with the Advice and Consent of the Senate, to make Treaties, provided two thirds of the Senators present concur; and he shall nominate, and by and with the Advice and Consent of the Senate, shall appoint Ambassadors, other public Ministers and Consuls, Judges of the supreme Court, and all other Officers of the United States, whose Appointments are not herein otherwise provided for, and which shall be established by Law: but the Congress may by Law vest the Appointment of such inferior Officers, as they think proper, in the President alone, in the Courts of Law, or in the Heads of Departments.

The President shall have Power to fill up all Vacancies that may happen during the Recess of the Senate, by granting Commissions which shall expire at the End of their next Session.

Section. 3.

He shall from time to time give to the Congress Information of the State of the Union, and recommend to their Consideration such Measures as he shall judge necessary and expedient; he may, on extraordinary Occasions, convene both Houses, or either of them, and in Case of Disagreement between them, with Respect to the Time of Adjournment, he may adjourn them to such Time as he shall think proper; he shall receive Ambassadors and other public Ministers; he shall take Care that

For a free Pocket Constitution, see <www.TCNPocket.com>.

the Laws be faithfully executed, and shall Commission all the Officers of the United States.

Section. 4.

The President, Vice President and all civil Officers of the United States, shall be removed from Office on Impeachment for, and Conviction of, Treason, Bribery, or other high Crimes and Misdemeanors.

Article. III.

Section. 1.

The judicial Power of the United States shall be vested in one supreme Court, and in such inferior Courts as the Congress may from time to time ordain and establish. The Judges, both of the supreme and inferior Courts, shall hold their Offices during good Behaviour, and shall, at stated Times, receive for their Services a Compensation, which shall not be diminished during their Continuance in Office.

Section. 2.

The judicial Power shall extend to all Cases, in Law and Equity, arising under this Constitution, the Laws of the United States, and Treaties made, or which shall be made, under their Authority;—to all Cases affecting Ambassadors, other public Ministers and Consuls;—to all Cases of admiralty and maritime Jurisdiction;—to Controversies to which the United States shall be a Party;—to Controversies between two or more States;— between a State and Citizens of another State,—between Citizens of different States,—between Citizens of the same State claiming Lands under Grants of different States, and between a State, or the Citizens thereof, and foreign States, Citizens or Subjects.

In all Cases affecting Ambassadors, other public Ministers and Consuls, and those in which a State shall be Party, the supreme Court shall have original Jurisdiction. In all the other Cases before mentioned, the supreme Court shall have appellate Jurisdiction, both as to Law and Fact, with such Exceptions, and under such Regulations as the Congress shall make.

The Trial of all Crimes, except in Cases of Impeachment, shall be by Jury; and such Trial shall be held in the State where the said Crimes shall have been committed; but when not committed within any State, the Trial shall be at such Place or Places as the Congress may by Law have directed.

For a free Pocket Constitution, see <www.TCNPocket.com>.

Section. 3.

Treason against the United States, shall consist only in levying War against them, or in adhering to their Enemies, giving them Aid and Comfort. No Person shall be convicted of Treason unless on the Testimony of two Witnesses to the same overt Act, or on Confession in open Court.

The Congress shall have Power to declare the Punishment of Treason, but no Attainder of Treason shall work Corruption of Blood, or Forfeiture except during the Life of the Person attainted.

Article. IV.

Section. 1.

Full Faith and Credit shall be given in each State to the public Acts, Records, and judicial Proceedings of every other State. And the Congress may by general Laws prescribe the Manner in which such Acts, Records and Proceedings shall be proved, and the Effect thereof.

Section. 2.

The Citizens of each State shall be entitled to all Privileges and Immunities of Citizens in the several States.

A Person charged in any State with Treason, Felony, or other Crime, who shall flee from Justice, and be found in another State, shall on Demand of the executive Authority of the State from which he fled, be delivered up, to be removed to the State having Jurisdiction of the Crime.

No Person held to Service or Labour in one State, under the Laws thereof, escaping into another, shall, in Consequence of any Law or Regulation therein, be discharged from such Service or Labour, but shall be delivered up on Claim of the Party to whom such Service or Labour may be due.

Section. 3.

New States may be admitted by the Congress into this Union; but no new State shall be formed or erected within the Jurisdiction of any other State; nor any State be formed by the Junction of two or more States, or Parts of States, without the Consent of the Legislatures of the States concerned as well as of the Congress.

The Congress shall have Power to dispose of and make all needful Rules and Regulations respecting the Territory or other Property belonging to the United States; and nothing in this Constitution shall be so

For a free Pocket Constitution, see <www.TCNPocket.com>.

construed as to Prejudice any Claims of the United States, or of any particular State.

Section. 4.

The United States shall guarantee to every State in this Union a Republican Form of Government, and shall protect each of them against Invasion; and on Application of the Legislature, or of the Executive (when the Legislature cannot be convened), against domestic Violence.

Article. V.

The Congress, whenever two thirds of both Houses shall deem it necessary, shall propose Amendments to this Constitution, or, on the Application of the Legislatures of two thirds of the several States, shall call a Convention for proposing Amendments, which, in either Case, shall be valid to all Intents and Purposes, as Part of this Constitution, when ratified by the Legislatures of three fourths of the several States, or by Conventions in three fourths thereof, as the one or the other Mode of Ratification may be proposed by the Congress; Provided that no Amendment which may be made prior to the Year One thousand eight hundred and eight shall in any Manner affect the first and fourth Clauses in the Ninth Section of the first Article; and that no State, without its Consent, shall be deprived of its equal Suffrage in the Senate.

Article. VI.

All Debts contracted and Engagements entered into, before the Adoption of this Constitution, shall be as valid against the United States under this Constitution, as under the Confederation.

This Constitution, and the Laws of the United States which shall be made in Pursuance thereof; and all Treaties made, or which shall be made, under the Authority of the United States, shall be the supreme Law of the Land; and the Judges in every State shall be bound thereby, any Thing in the Constitution or Laws of any State to the Contrary notwithstanding.

The Senators and Representatives before mentioned, and the Members of the several State Legislatures, and all executive and judicial Officers, both of the United States and of the several States, shall be bound by Oath or Affirmation, to support this Constitution; but no religious Test shall ever be required as a Qualification to any Office or public Trust under the United States.

For a free Pocket Constitution, see <www.TCNPocket.com>.

Article. VII.

The Ratification of the Conventions of nine States, shall be sufficient for the Establishment of this Constitution between the States so ratifying the Same.

The Word, "the," being interlined between the seventh and eighth Lines of the first Page, the Word "Thirty" being partly written on an Erazure in the fifteenth Line of the first Page, The Words "is tried" being interlined between the thirty second and thirty third Lines of the first Page and the Word "the" being interlined between the forty third and forty fourth Lines of the second Page.

Attest William Jackson Secretary

done in Convention by the Unanimous Consent of the States present the Seventeenth Day of September in the Year of our Lord one thousand seven hundred and Eighty seven and of the Independance of the United States of America the Twelfth In witness whereof We have hereunto subscribed our Names,

G°. Washington
Presidt and deputy
from Virginia

Delaware
Geo: Read
Gunning Bedford jun
John Dickinson
Richard Bassett
Jaco: Broom

Maryland
James McHenry
Dan of St Thos. Jenifer
Danl. Carroll

Virginia
John Blair
James Madison Jr.

North Carolina
Wm. Blount
Richd. Dobbs Spaight
Hu Williamson

South Carolina
J. Rutledge
Charles Cotesworth
Pinckney
Charles Pinckney
Pierce Butler

Georgia
William Few
Abr Baldwin

New Hampshire
John Langdon
Nicholas Gilman

Massachusetts
Nathaniel Gorham
Rufus King

Connecticut
Wm. Saml. Johnson
Roger Sherman

New York
Alexander Hamilton

New Jersey
Wil: Livingston
David Brearley
Wm. Paterson
Jona: Dayton

Pennsylvania
B Franklin
Thomas Mifflin
Robt. Morris
Geo. Clymer
Thos. FitzSimons
Jared Ingersoll
James Wilson
Gouv Morris

For a free Pocket Constitution, see <www.TCNPocket.com>.

The Bill of Rights

The Preamble to The Bill of Rights

Congress of the United States
begun and held at the City of New-York,
on Wednesday the fourth of March,
one thousand seven hundred and eighty nine.

THE Conventions of a number of the States, having at the time of their adopting the Constitution, expressed a desire, in order to prevent misconstruction or abuse of its powers, that further declaratory and restrictive clauses should be added: And as extending the ground of public confidence in the Government, will best ensure the beneficent ends of its institution.

RESOLVED by the Senate and House of Representatives of the United States of America, in Congress assembled, two thirds of both Houses concurring, that the following Articles be proposed to the Legislatures of the several States, as amendments to the Constitution of the United States, all, or any of which Articles, when ratified by three fourths of the said Legislatures, to be valid to all intents and purposes, as part of the said Constitution; viz.

ARTICLES in addition to, and Amendment of the Constitution of the United States of America, proposed by Congress, and ratified by the Legislatures of the several States, pursuant to the fifth Article of the original Constitution.

Note: *The following text is a transcription of the first ten amendments to the Constitution in their original form. These amendments were ratified December 15, 1791, and form what is known as the "Bill of Rights."*

Amendment I

Congress shall make no law respecting an establishment of religion, or prohibiting the free exercise thereof; or abridging the freedom of

For a free Pocket Constitution, see <www.TCNPocket.com>.

speech, or of the press; or the right of the people peaceably to assemble, and to petition the Government for a redress of grievances.

Amendment II

A well regulated Militia, being necessary to the security of a free State, the right of the people to keep and bear Arms, shall not be infringed.

Amendment III

No Soldier shall, in time of peace be quartered in any house, without the consent of the Owner, nor in time of war, but in a manner to be prescribed by law.

Amendment IV

The right of the people to be secure in their persons, houses, papers, and effects, against unreasonable searches and seizures, shall not be violated, and no Warrants shall issue, but upon probable cause, supported by Oath or affirmation, and particularly describing the place to be searched, and the persons or things to be seized.

Amendment V

No person shall be held to answer for a capital, or otherwise infamous crime, unless on a presentment or indictment of a Grand Jury, except in cases arising in the land or naval forces, or in the Militia, when in actual service in time of War or public danger; nor shall any person be subject for the same offence to be twice put in jeopardy of life or limb; nor shall be compelled in any criminal case to be a witness against himself, nor be deprived of life, liberty, or property, without due process of law; nor shall private property be taken for public use, without just compensation.

Amendment VI

In all criminal prosecutions, the accused shall enjoy the right to a speedy and public trial, by an impartial jury of the State and district wherein the crime shall have been committed, which district shall have been previously ascertained by law, and to be informed of the nature and cause of the accusation; to be confronted with the witnesses against him; to have compulsory process for obtaining witnesses in his favor, and to have the Assistance of Counsel for his defence.

For a free Pocket Constitution, see <www.TCNPocket.com>.

Amendment VII

In Suits at common law, where the value in controversy shall exceed twenty dollars, the right of trial by jury shall be preserved, and no fact tried by a jury, shall be otherwise re-examined in any Court of the United States, than according to the rules of the common law.

Amendment VIII

Excessive bail shall not be required, nor excessive fines imposed, nor cruel and unusual punishments inflicted.

Amendment IX

The enumeration in the Constitution, of certain rights, shall not be construed to deny or disparage others retained by the people.

Amendment X

The powers not delegated to the United States by the Constitution, nor prohibited by it to the States, are reserved to the States respectively, or to the people.

For a free Pocket Constitution, see <www.TCNPocket.com>.

Amendments XI–XXVII

Amendment XI

Passed by Congress March 4, 1794.
Ratified February 7, 1795.
Note: Article III, section 2, of the Constitution
was modified by amendment 11.

The Judicial power of the United States shall not be construed to extend to any suit in law or equity, commenced or prosecuted against one of the United States by Citizens of another State, or by Citizens or Subjects of any Foreign State.

Amendment XII

Passed by Congress December 9, 1803.
Ratified June 15, 1804.
Note: A portion of Article II, section 1 of the
Constitution was superseded by the 12th amendment.

The Electors shall meet in their respective states and vote by ballot for President and Vice-President, one of whom, at least, shall not be an inhabitant of the same state with themselves; they shall name in their ballots the person voted for as President, and in distinct ballots the person voted for as Vice-President, and they shall make distinct lists of all persons voted for as President, and of all persons voted for as Vice-President, and of the number of votes for each, which lists they shall sign and certify, and transmit sealed to the seat of the government of the United States, directed to the President of the Senate; —the President of the Senate shall, in the presence of the Senate and House of Representatives, open all the certificates and the votes shall then be counted; —The person having the greatest number of votes for President, shall be the President, if such number be a majority of the whole number of Electors appointed; and if no person have such majority, then from the persons having the highest numbers not exceeding three on the list of those voted for as President, the House of Representatives shall choose immediately, by ballot, the President. But in choosing the President, the votes shall be taken by states, the representation from each state having one vote; a quorum for this purpose shall consist of a member or

For a free Pocket Constitution, see <www.TCNPocket.com>.

members from two-thirds of the states, and a majority of all the states shall be necessary to a choice. [And if the House of Representatives shall not choose a President whenever the right of choice shall devolve upon them, before the fourth day of March next following, then the Vice-President shall act as President, as in case of the death or other constitutional disability of the President. —]* The person having the greatest number of votes as Vice-President, shall be the Vice-President, if such number be a majority of the whole number of Electors appointed, and if no person have a majority, then from the two highest numbers on the list, the Senate shall choose the Vice-President; a quorum for the purpose shall consist of two-thirds of the whole number of Senators, and a majority of the whole number shall be necessary to a choice. But no person constitutionally ineligible to the office of President shall be eligible to that of Vice-President of the United States.
Superseded by section 3 of the 20th amendment.

Amendment XIII

Passed by Congress January 31, 1865.
Ratified December 6, 1865.
Note: A portion of Article IV, section 2, of the Constitution
was superseded by the 13th amendment.

Section 1.

Neither slavery nor involuntary servitude, except as a punishment for crime whereof the party shall have been duly convicted, shall exist within the United States, or any place subject to their jurisdiction.

Section 2.

Congress shall have power to enforce this article by appropriate legislation.

Amendment XIV

Passed by Congress June 13, 1866.
Ratified July 9, 1868.
Note: Article I, section 2, of the Constitution
was modified by section 2 of the 14th amendment.

Section 1.

All persons born or naturalized in the United States, and subject to the jurisdiction thereof, are citizens of the United States and of the State wherein they reside. No State shall make or enforce any law which shall abridge the privileges or immunities of citizens of the United States; nor shall any State deprive any person of life, liberty, or property, without due process of law; nor deny to any person within its jurisdiction the equal protection of the laws.

Section 2.

Representatives shall be apportioned among the several States according to their respective numbers, counting the whole number of persons in each State, excluding Indians not taxed. But when the right to vote at any election for the choice of electors for President and Vice-President of the United States, Representatives in Congress, the Executive and Judicial officers of a State, or the members of the Legislature thereof, is denied to any of the male inhabitants of such State, being twenty-one years of age,* and citizens of the United States, or in any way abridged, except for participation in rebellion, or other crime, the basis of representation therein shall be reduced in the proportion which the number of such male citizens shall bear to the whole number of male citizens twenty-one years of age in such State.

Section 3.

No person shall be a Senator or Representative in Congress, or elector of President and Vice-President, or hold any office, civil or military, under the United States, or under any State, who, having previously taken an oath, as a member of Congress, or as an officer of the United States, or as a member of any State legislature, or as an executive or judicial officer of any State, to support the Constitution of the United States, shall have engaged in insurrection or rebellion against the same, or given aid or comfort to the enemies thereof. But Congress may by a vote of two-thirds of each House, remove such disability.

Section 4.

The validity of the public debt of the United States, authorized by law, including debts incurred for payment of pensions and bounties for services in suppressing insurrection or rebellion, shall not be questioned. But neither the United States nor any State shall assume or pay any debt or obligation incurred in aid of insurrection or rebellion against the United States, or any claim for the loss or emancipation of any slave; but all such debts, obligations and claims shall be held illegal and void.

For a free Pocket Constitution, see <www.TCNPocket.com>.

Section 5.

The Congress shall have the power to enforce, by appropriate legislation, the provisions of this article.

Changed by section 1 of the 26th amendment.

Amendment XV

Passed by Congress February 26, 1869.
Ratified February 3, 1870.

Section 1.

The right of citizens of the United States to vote shall not be denied or abridged by the United States or by any State on account of race, color, or previous condition of servitude—

Section 2.

The Congress shall have the power to enforce this article by appropriate legislation.

Amendment XVI

Passed by Congress July 2, 1909.
Ratified February 3, 1913.
Note: Article I, section 9, of the Constitution
was modified by amendment 16.

The Congress shall have power to lay and collect taxes on incomes, from whatever source derived, without apportionment among the several States, and without regard to any census or enumeration.

Amendment XVII

Passed by Congress May 13, 1912.
Ratified April 8, 1913.
Note: Article I, section 3, of the Constitution
was modified by the 17th amendment.

The Senate of the United States shall be composed of two Senators from each State, elected by the people thereof, for six years; and each Senator shall have one vote. The electors in each State shall have the qualifications requisite for electors of the most numerous branch of the State legislatures.

When vacancies happen in the representation of any State in the Senate, the executive authority of such State shall issue writs of elec-

For a free Pocket Constitution, see <www.TCNPocket.com>.

tion to fill such vacancies: Provided, That the legislature of any State may empower the executive thereof to make temporary appointments until the people fill the vacancies by election as the legislature may direct.

This amendment shall not be so construed as to affect the election or term of any Senator chosen before it becomes valid as part of the Constitution.

Amendment XVIII

Passed by Congress December 18, 1917.
Ratified January 16, 1919.
Repealed by amendment 21.

Section 1.

After one year from the ratification of this article the manufacture, sale, or transportation of intoxicating liquors within, the importation thereof into, or the exportation thereof from the United States and all territory subject to the jurisdiction thereof for beverage purposes is hereby prohibited.

Section 2.

The Congress and the several States shall have concurrent power to enforce this article by appropriate legislation.

Section 3.

This article shall be inoperative unless it shall have been ratified as an amendment to the Constitution by the legislatures of the several States, as provided in the Constitution, within seven years from the date of the submission hereof to the States by the Congress.

Amendment XIX

Passed by Congress June 4, 1919.
Ratified August 18, 1920.

The right of citizens of the United States to vote shall not be denied or abridged by the United States or by any State on account of sex.

Congress shall have power to enforce this article by appropriate legislation.

For a free Pocket Constitution, see <www.TCNPocket.com>.

Amendment XX

Passed by Congress March 2, 1932.
Ratified January 23, 1933.
Note: Article I, section 4, of the Constitution
was modified by section 2 of this amendment. In addition,
a portion of the 12th amendment was superseded by section 3.

Section 1.

The terms of the President and the Vice President shall end at noon on the 20th day of January, and the terms of Senators and Representatives at noon on the 3d day of January, of the years in which such terms would have ended if this article had not been ratified; and the terms of their successors shall then begin.

Section 2.

The Congress shall assemble at least once in every year, and such meeting shall begin at noon on the 3d day of January, unless they shall by law appoint a different day.

Section 3.

If, at the time fixed for the beginning of the term of the President, the President elect shall have died, the Vice President elect shall become President. If a President shall not have been chosen before the time fixed for the beginning of his term, or if the President elect shall have failed to qualify, then the Vice President elect shall act as President until a President shall have qualified; and the Congress may by law provide for the case wherein neither a President elect nor a Vice President shall have qualified, declaring who shall then act as President, or the manner in which one who is to act shall be selected, and such person shall act accordingly until a President or Vice President shall have qualified.

Section 4.

The Congress may by law provide for the case of the death of any of the persons from whom the House of Representatives may choose a President whenever the right of choice shall have devolved upon them, and for the case of the death of any of the persons from whom the Senate may choose a Vice President whenever the right of choice shall have devolved upon them.

For a free Pocket Constitution, see <www.TCNPocket.com>.

Section 5.

Sections 1 and 2 shall take effect on the 15th day of October following the ratification of this article.

Section 6.

This article shall be inoperative unless it shall have been ratified as an amendment to the Constitution by the legislatures of three-fourths of the several States within seven years from the date of its submission.

Amendment XXI

Passed by Congress February 20, 1933.
Ratified December 5, 1933.

Section 1.

The eighteenth article of amendment to the Constitution of the United States is hereby repealed.

Section 2.

The transportation or importation into any State, Territory, or Possession of the United States for delivery or use therein of intoxicating liquors, in violation of the laws thereof, is hereby prohibited.

Section 3.

This article shall be inoperative unless it shall have been ratified as an amendment to the Constitution by conventions in the several States, as provided in the Constitution, within seven years from the date of the submission hereof to the States by the Congress.

Amendment XXII

Passed by Congress March 21, 1947.
Ratified February 27, 1951.

Section 1.

No person shall be elected to the office of the President more than twice, and no person who has held the office of President, or acted as President, for more than two years of a term to which some other person was elected President shall be elected to the office of President more than once. But this Article shall not apply to any person holding the office of President when this Article was proposed by Congress, and shall not prevent any person who may be holding the office of Pres-

For a free Pocket Constitution, see <www.TCNPocket.com>.

ident, or acting as President, during the term within which this Article becomes operative from holding the office of President or acting as President during the remainder of such term.

Section 2.

This article shall be inoperative unless it shall have been ratified as an amendment to the Constitution by the legislatures of three-fourths of the several States within seven years from the date of its submission to the States by the Congress.

Amendment XXIII

Passed by Congress June 16, 1960.
Ratified March 29, 1961.

Section 1.

The District constituting the seat of Government of the United States shall appoint in such manner as Congress may direct:

A number of electors of President and Vice President equal to the whole number of Senators and Representatives in Congress to which the District would be entitled if it were a State, but in no event more than the least populous State; they shall be in addition to those appointed by the States, but they shall be considered, for the purposes of the election of President and Vice President, to be electors appointed by a State; and they shall meet in the District and perform such duties as provided by the twelfth article of amendment.

Section 2.

The Congress shall have power to enforce this article by appropriate legislation.

Amendment XXIV

Passed by Congress August 27, 1962.
Ratified January 23, 1964.

Section 1.

The right of citizens of the United States to vote in any primary or other election for President or Vice President, for electors for President or Vice President, or for Senator or Representative in Congress, shall not be denied or abridged by the United States or any State by reason of failure to pay poll tax or other tax.

For a free Pocket Constitution, see <www.TCNPocket.com>.

Section 2.

The Congress shall have power to enforce this article by appropriate legislation.

Amendment XXV

Passed by Congress July 6, 1965.
Ratified February 10, 1967.
Note: Article II, section 1, of the Constitution
was affected by the 25th amendment.

Section 1.

In case of the removal of the President from office or of his death or resignation, the Vice President shall become President.

Section 2.

Whenever there is a vacancy in the office of the Vice President, the President shall nominate a Vice President who shall take office upon confirmation by a majority vote of both Houses of Congress.

Section 3.

Whenever the President transmits to the President pro tempore of the Senate and the Speaker of the House of Representatives his written declaration that he is unable to discharge the powers and duties of his office, and until he transmits to them a written declaration to the contrary, such powers and duties shall be discharged by the Vice President as Acting President.

Section 4.

Whenever the Vice President and a majority of either the principal officers of the executive departments or of such other body as Congress may by law provide, transmit to the President pro tempore of the Senate and the Speaker of the House of Representatives their written declaration that the President is unable to discharge the powers and duties of his office, the Vice President shall immediately assume the powers and duties of the office as Acting President.

Thereafter, when the President transmits to the President pro tempore of the Senate and the Speaker of the House of Representatives his written declaration that no inability exists, he shall resume the powers and duties of his office unless the Vice President and a majority of ei-

For a free Pocket Constitution, see <www.TCNPocket.com>.

ther the principal officers of the executive department or of such other body as Congress may by law provide, transmit within four days to the President pro tempore of the Senate and the Speaker of the House of Representatives their written declaration that the President is unable to discharge the powers and duties of his office. Thereupon Congress shall decide the issue, assembling within forty-eight hours for that purpose if not in session. If the Congress, within twenty-one days after receipt of the latter written declaration, or, if Congress is not in session, within twenty-one days after Congress is required to assemble, determines by two-thirds vote of both Houses that the President is unable to discharge the powers and duties of his office, the Vice President shall continue to discharge the same as Acting President; otherwise, the President shall resume the powers and duties of his office.

Amendment XXVI

Passed by Congress March 23, 1971.
Ratified July 1, 1971.
Note: Amendment 14, section 2, of the Constitution
was modified by section 1 of the 26th amendment.

Section 1.

The right of citizens of the United States, who are eighteen years of age or older, to vote shall not be denied or abridged by the United States or by any State on account of age.

Section 2.

The Congress shall have power to enforce this article by appropriate legislation.

Amendment XXVII

Originally proposed Sept. 25, 1789.
Ratified May 7, 1992.

No law, varying the compensation for the services of the Senators and Representatives, shall take effect, until an election of representatives shall have intervened.

For a free Pocket Constitution, see <www.TCNPocket.com>.

Appendix B
The Declaration of Independence

IN CONGRESS, July 4, 1776.

The unanimous Declaration of the thirteen united States of America,

When in the Course of human events, it becomes necessary for one people to dissolve the political bands which have connected them with another, and to assume among the powers of the earth, the separate and equal station to which the Laws of Nature and of Nature's God entitle them, a decent respect to the opinions of mankind requires that they should declare the causes which impel them to the separation.

We hold these truths to be self-evident, that all men are created equal, that they are endowed by their Creator with certain unalienable Rights, that among these are Life, Liberty and the pursuit of Happiness.—That to secure these rights, Governments are instituted among Men, deriving their just powers from the consent of the governed,—That whenever any Form of Government becomes destructive of these ends, it is the Right of the People to alter or to abolish it, and to institute new Government, laying its foundation on such principles and organizing its powers in such form, as to them shall seem most likely to effect their Safety and Happiness. Prudence, indeed, will dictate that Governments long established should not be changed for light and transient causes; and accordingly all experience hath shewn, that mankind are more disposed to suffer, while evils are sufferable, than to right themselves by abolishing the forms to which they are accustomed. But when a long train of abuses and usurpations, pursuing invariably the same Object evinces a design to reduce them under absolute Despotism, it is their right, it is their duty, to throw off such Government, and to provide new Guards for their future security.—Such has been the patient sufferance of these Colonies; and such is now the necessity which constrains them to alter their former Systems of Government. The history of the present King of Great Britain is a history of repeated injuries and usurpations, all having in direct object the establishment of an absolute Tyranny over these States. To prove this, let Facts be submitted to a candid world.

For a free Pocket Constitution, see <www.TCNPocket.com>.

He has refused his Assent to Laws, the most wholesome and necessary for the public good.

He has forbidden his Governors to pass Laws of immediate and pressing importance, unless suspended in their operation till his Assent should be obtained; and when so suspended, he has utterly neglected to attend to them.

He has refused to pass other Laws for the accommodation of large districts of people, unless those people would relinquish the right of Representation in the Legislature, a right inestimable to them and formidable to tyrants only.

He has called together legislative bodies at places unusual, uncomfortable, and distant from the depository of their public Records, for the sole purpose of fatiguing them into compliance with his measures.

He has dissolved Representative Houses repeatedly, for opposing with manly firmness his invasions on the rights of the people.

He has refused for a long time, after such dissolutions, to cause others to be elected; whereby the Legislative powers, incapable of Annihilation, have returned to the People at large for their exercise; the State remaining in the mean time exposed to all the dangers of invasion from without, and convulsions within.

He has endeavoured to prevent the population of these States; for that purpose obstructing the Laws for Naturalization of Foreigners; refusing to pass others to encourage their migrations hither, and raising the conditions of new Appropriations of Lands.

He has obstructed the Administration of Justice, by refusing his Assent to Laws for establishing Judiciary powers.

He has made Judges dependent on his Will alone, for the tenure of their offices, and the amount and payment of their salaries.

He has erected a multitude of New Offices, and sent hither swarms of Officers to harrass our people, and eat out their substance.

He has kept among us, in times of peace, Standing Armies without the Consent of our legislatures.

For a free Pocket Constitution, see <www.TCNPocket.com>.

He has affected to render the Military independent of and superior to the Civil power.

He has combined with others to subject us to a jurisdiction foreign to our constitution, and unacknowledged by our laws; giving his Assent to their Acts of pretended Legislation:

For Quartering large bodies of armed troops among us:

For protecting them, by a mock Trial, from punishment for any Murders which they should commit on the Inhabitants of these States:

For cutting off our Trade with all parts of the world:

For imposing Taxes on us without our Consent:

For depriving us in many cases, of the benefits of Trial by Jury:

For transporting us beyond Seas to be tried for pretended offences

For abolishing the free System of English Laws in a neighbouring Province, establishing therein an Arbitrary government, and enlarging its Boundaries so as to render it at once an example and fit instrument for introducing the same absolute rule into these Colonies:

For taking away our Charters, abolishing our most valuable Laws, and altering fundamentally the Forms of our Governments:

For suspending our own Legislatures, and declaring themselves invested with power to legislate for us in all cases whatsoever.

He has abdicated Government here, by declaring us out of his Protection and waging War against us.

He has plundered our seas, ravaged our Coasts, burnt our towns, and destroyed the lives of our people.

He is at this time transporting large Armies of foreign Mercenaries to compleat the works of death, desolation and tyranny, already begun with circumstances of Cruelty & perfidy scarcely paralleled in the most barbarous ages, and totally unworthy the Head of a civilized nation.

For a free Pocket Constitution, see <www.TCNPocket.com>.

He has constrained our fellow Citizens taken Captive on the high Seas to bear Arms against their Country, to become the executioners of their friends and Brethren, or to fall themselves by their Hands.

He has excited domestic insurrections amongst us, and has endeavoured to bring on the inhabitants of our frontiers, the merciless Indian Savages, whose known rule of warfare, is an undistinguished destruction of all ages, sexes and conditions.

In every stage of these Oppressions We have Petitioned for Redress in the most humble terms: Our repeated Petitions have been answered only by repeated injury. A Prince whose character is thus marked by every act which may define a Tyrant, is unfit to be the ruler of a free people.

Nor have We been wanting in attentions to our Brittish brethren. We have warned them from time to time of attempts by their legislature to extend an unwarrantable jurisdiction over us. We have reminded them of the circumstances of our emigration and settlement here. We have appealed to their native justice and magnanimity, and we have conjured them by the ties of our common kindred to disavow these usurpations, which, would inevitably interrupt our connections and correspondence. They too have been deaf to the voice of justice and of consanguinity. We must, therefore, acquiesce in the necessity, which denounces our Separation, and hold them, as we hold the rest of mankind, Enemies in War, in Peace Friends.

We, therefore, the Representatives of the united States of America, in General Congress, Assembled, appealing to the Supreme Judge of the world for the rectitude of our intentions, do, in the Name, and by Authority of the good People of these Colonies, solemnly publish and declare, That these United Colonies are, and of Right ought to be Free and Independent States; that they are Absolved from all Allegiance to the British Crown, and that all political connection between them and the State of Great Britain, is and ought to be totally dissolved; and that as Free and Independent States, they have full Power to levy War, conclude Peace, contract Alliances, establish Commerce, and to do all other Acts and Things which Independent States may of right do. And

For a free Pocket Constitution, see <www.TCNPocket.com>.

for the support of this Declaration, with a firm reliance on the protection of divine Providence, we mutually pledge to each other our Lives, our Fortunes and our sacred Honor.

Georgia
Button Gwinnett
Lyman Hall
George Walton

North Carolina
William Hooper
Joseph Hewes
John Penn

South Carolina
Edward Rutledge
Thomas Heyward, Jr.
Thomas Lynch, Jr.
Arthur Middleton

Massachusetts
John Hancock

Maryland
Samuel Chase
William Paca
Thomas Stone
Charles Carroll
of Carrollton

Virginia
George Wythe
Richard Henry Lee
Thomas Jefferson
Benjamin Harrison
Thomas Nelson, Jr.
Francis Lightfoot Lee
Carter Braxton

Pennsylvania
Robert Morris
Benjamin Rush
Benjamin Franklin
John Morton
George Clymer
James Smith
George Taylor
James Wilson
George Ross

Delaware
Caesar Rodney
George Read
Thomas McKean

New York
William Floyd
Philip Livingston
Francis Lewis
Lewis Morris

New Jersey
Richard Stockton
John Witherspoon
Francis Hopkinson
John Hart
Abraham Clark

New Hampshire
Josiah Bartlett
William Whipple

Massachusetts
Samuel Adams
John Adams
Robert Treat Paine
Elbridge Gerry

Rhode Island
Stephen Hopkins
William Ellery

Connecticut
Roger Sherman
Samuel Huntington
William Williams
Oliver Wolcott

New Hampshire
Matthew Thornton

For a free Pocket Constitution, see <www.TCNPocket.com>.

Appendix C
The Advocate's Pledge

Stating the following boldface sentences—out loud and in front of your colleagues—will increase the likelihood that you and your colleagues will actually *commit* and follow through.

- **Article 1: I will politely petition my legislator with all appropriate measures.** This pushes advocates to be well-mannered and rational in their dealings with legislators and to use every available means to influence policy (including in-person meetings, email, and attendance at town hall meetings).

- **Article 2: Under the Constitution, my legislator must listen to me . . . but I must still know what I'm talking about.** Yes, according to the First Amendment, advocates have a right to petition the government for a "redress of grievances." But if advocates want government to respond in the desired manner, they must know the issues and clearly communicate the impact of what they desire for a community, an interest group, or industry.

- **Article 3: I will encourage my fellow citizens to aid in our cause.** The Internet now makes creating networks easier than ever. Nearly every type of grassroots software available has a tell-a-friend feature that allows users to build connections instantly.

- **Article 4: Success is realized in both the result and in my participation in the democratic process.** Of course, winning is better than losing. But just because advocates suffer defeat with one legislative battle doesn't mean they're out of the game forever. It takes an average of seven years to pass a bill into law. Patience is more than a virtue . . . it's a requirement.

What's more, by participating in the democratic process, you send an important message to your member of Congress: "I'm watching." Accountability is the foundation of democracy. Just by being involved, you make a difference.

Appendix D
How to Analyze a Legislator's Perception of Our Issue

Every politician analyzes requests for his assistance through his own prism. He asks himself a series of questions when analyzing an issue. Understanding a legislator's thinking process is valuable in developing your strategy. Below are a series of questions designed to help you look at your issue the way a legislator does.

1. What do we want the legislator to do?

   * Identify a specific request of the legislator. It is crucial that advocates have a specific measurement by which to hold the legislator accountable.

2. What is the legislator's history with this issue?

   * Politicians are slaves to consistency. They know that changing a position will result in withering criticism as a "flip-flopper" by the media and political opponents. It is significantly easier to win over an undecided legislator than to convert a committed one. Understanding your legislator's history is the starting point for developing an influence strategy.

3. Why would the legislator care about our issue? Does it connect to the legislator's goals or does it impact the legislator's re-election?

   * Politicians are rather predictable creatures who behave according to their values and political instincts. By researching the legislator, her priorities, and the political make-up of the district or state, you can identify reasonable motivation for her to support your cause.

4. What are our influence strengths? What tools/assets are most persuasive and helpful to gaining the legislator's support?

- Every constituent group has some degree of political clout. Legislators keep a mental tally (some keep a written one) of groups that are important to them politically. Identify your group's strengths. It is important to *quantify* the strength: through membership roles, contribution to the economy, number of VIPs who can call the legislator or senior staff— any factor that could be used for influence.

5. What are our influence liabilities? Will the legislator need to spend political capital to support us? Are there negative repercussions if the legislator supports us?

- Legislators want constituent groups to understand *their* problems. Successful groups and lobbyists always appreciate the challenges and pressures that legislators feel, and seek ways to mitigate the political damage they may incur through supporting your cause.

6. Who are our allies? Are there other groups we can coordinate with to amplify our message?

- Rare is the cause that does not have multiple supporters. Identify other groups or local VIPs who share your cause. Coordinate on timing and message to enhance your strength and image.

7. What other groups are involved in this issue and how do they relate to our position? Do we have active opposition, or just competition for resources?

- Every constituent group has competition, even if it is just for the legislator's precious time and resources. Identify groups that might be opposing you or may be seeking precious appropriations dollars from the same pot of money.

8. How do we maximize our influence strengths?

   * To enhance influence strengths, can we bolster supporters, add credibility to the case with third-party endorsements, build partnerships with other groups to demonstrate diversity of support for our position?

9. How do we minimize our influence liabilities?

   * To minimize liabilities, can we neutralize arguments through communications strategies (online, free and paid media), discredit opponents' motives, or offer the legislator some measurement that illustrates minimal impact to his image?

10. How best can we connect with the legislator?

   * After identifying allies, opponents, strengths, and weaknesses, what is the best influence strategy? What is the best combination of tactics, messages, and influence factors that is most likely to win her over?

Appendix E
How Legislators Perceive Issues

POLICY

POLITICS

	Connected to Legislator's Goals/ Consistent with Values	**Not Connected to Legislator's Goals/Not Consistent with Values**
Important to Constituents	• Issues/Projects that Impact Local Economy • Issues/Projects that Impact or Interest Many Constituents • Issues/Projects that Have Significant Impact on State or Nation	• Issues/Projects Important to Key Political Supporters • Issues/Projects Important to Elected Officials • Issues/Projects with Significant Coalition Support
Not Important to Constituents	• Issues/Projects with Personal Connection to Legislator • Issues/Projects on which Legislator Wishes to Demonstrate Leadership or Associate with	• Issues/Projects Important to Groups/Individuals Not Central to Legislator's Goals or Re-Election • Issues/Projects without Clear Connection to Congressional District

Appendix F
Information about Congress and Washington, DC

- Capitol Switchboard
  202-224-3121

- House of Representatives
  <*www.house.gov*>

- Senate
  <*www.senate.gov*>

- White House
  <*www.whitehouse.gov*>
  202-456-1414

- Congress Seating Charts
  <*www.CongressSeating.com*>

- Congressional Leadership
  and Committees
  <*www.CongressLeaders.com*>

- Current party numbers in
  Congress and Differences
  between the House and
  the Senate At-a-Glance
  <*www.CongressBy
  TheNumbers.com*>

- Glossary of congressional terms
  <*www.Congressional
  Glossary.com*>

- Pay and perquisites
  of Members of Congress
  <*www.CongressPay.com*>

- Terms of Congress
  <*www.TermsofCongress.com*>

- Visiting Washington, DC page
  <*www.TCNDC.com*>

Publications from TheCapitol.Net

- *Congressional
  Deskbook, The Practical
  and Comprehensive
  Guide to Congress,*
  by Michael Koempel
  and Judy Schneider
  <*www.Congressional
  Deskbook.com*>

- Congressional
  Operations Poster
  <*www.Congress
  Poster.com*>

- *Lobbying and Advocacy,*
  by Deanna Gelak
  <*www.Lobbyingand
  Advocacy.com*>

- *Persuading Congress,*
  by Joseph Gibson
  <*www.Persuading
  Congress.com*>

- *Testifying
  Before Congress,*
  by William LaForge
  <*www.TestifyingBefore
  Congress.com*>

- The Federal
  Budget Process
  <*www.FederalBudget
  Process.com*>

Appendix G
Legislative Process Flowchart

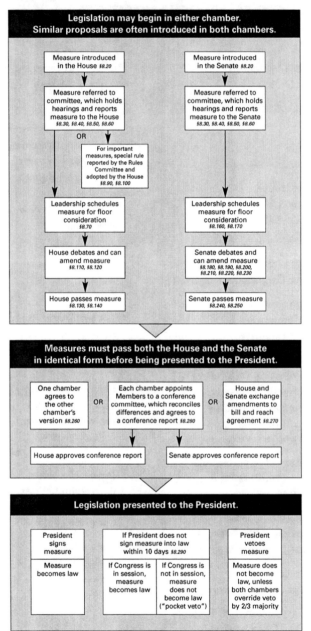

**Legislation may begin in either chamber.
Similar proposals are often introduced in both chambers.**

Measure introduced in the House *§8.20*	Measure introduced in the Senate *§8.20*
Measure referred to committee, which holds hearings and reports measure to the House *§8.30, §8.40, §8.50, §8.60*	Measure referred to committee, which holds hearings and reports measure to the Senate *§8.30, §8.40, §8.50, §8.60*

OR

For important measures, special rule reported by the Rules Committee and adopted by the House *§8.90, §8.100*

Leadership schedules measure for floor consideration *§8.70*	Leadership schedules measure for floor consideration *§8.160, §8.170*
House debates and can amend measure *§8.110, §8.120*	Senate debates and can amend measure *§8.180, §8.190, §8.200, §8.210, §8.220, §8.230*
House passes measure *§8.130, §8.140*	Senate passes measure *§8.240, §8.250*

**Measures must pass both the House and the Senate
in identical form before being presented to the President.**

One chamber agrees to the other chamber's version *§8.260*	OR	Each chamber appoints Members to a conference committee, which reconciles differences and agrees to a conference report *§8.280*	OR	House and Senate exchange amendments to bill and reach agreement *§8.270*

House approves conference report	Senate approves conference report

Legislation presented to the President.

President signs measure	If President does not sign measure into law within 10 days *§8.290*		President vetoes measure
Measure becomes law	If Congress is in session, measure becomes law	If Congress is not in session, measure does not become law ("pocket veto")	Measure does not become law, unless both chambers override veto by 2/3 majority

Sources: U.S. Senate; U.S. House of Representatives; and the Congressional Deskbook by Michael Koempel and Judy Schneider. Copyright ©2009 by TheCapitol.Net, Inc. All Rights Reserved. 202-678-1600 www.TheCapitol.Net

Appendix H
State and Local Resources

State and Local Government

- State and Local Government on the Net
  <www.statelocalgov.net>
- State Government
  <www.govspot.com/state>
- State Government
  <www.apl.org/quick/state.html>
- State Legislatures, State Laws and State Regulations:
  Web Site Links and Telephone Numbers
  <www.llsdc.org/sourcebook/state-leg>

State and Local Newspapers

- U.S. Newspapers, by state
  <www.usnpl.com>
- U.S. Newspapers, by state
  <www.onlinenewspapers.com/usstate/usatable.htm>

Associations

- National Association of Counties (NACO)
  <www.naco.org>
- National Conference of State Legislatures (NCSL)
  <www.ncsl.org>
- National Governors Association (NGA)
  <www.nga.org>
- National League of Cities (NLC)
  <www.nlc.org>
- The United States Conference of Mayors
  <www.usmayors.org>

Epilogue

Great leaders understand that the ultimate power in a democracy rests with the people, not with congressmen or presidents or the special interest lobbyists. "Public sentiment is everything," President Abraham Lincoln said. "With public sentiment, nothing can fail, without it, nothing can succeed." The next time you want to rant at something the government has done, remember Lincoln's words and don't just rant. Pick up a pen, call a friend, or send an email. Give purpose to your passion, knowing that you and others like you have the power to change the world. Remember Margaret Mead: "Never doubt that a small group of committed citizens can change the world . . . indeed, it is the only thing that ever has."

About the Author

Bradford Fitch has spent 25 years in Washington as a journalist, congressional aide, consultant, college instructor, and writer/researcher. After working as a radio and television reporter in the mid-1980s, Fitch began working on Capitol Hill in 1988. During his 13 years on Capitol Hill he served in a variety of positions for four members of Congress including: press secretary, legislative director, and chief of staff.

In 2001 Fitch left Capitol Hill to become Deputy Director of the Congressional Management Foundation, an organization that advises congressional offices on how to improve operations. In 2006 Fitch cofounded Knowlegis, which provides data and software services to associations, nonprofits, and lobbyists. In 2010 he returned to the Congressional Management Foundation as President and CEO.

He is the author of *Media Relations Handbook for Agencies, Associations, Nonprofits, and Congress*, <*www.TheCapitol.Net*>, a guide for public relations professionals in the public affairs community.

Fitch has served as an adjunct Associate Professor at American University's School of Communication. He received his BA in Political Science from Johns Hopkins University and his MA in Journalism and Public Affairs from American University.

Index

Communications Director, 18

Competition for influence over legislative decision-making, 33

Congressional Accountability Act, 12

Congressional culture, 11–19
  committees, 13–15
  power hierarchy, 13
  staff hierarchy, 15–19
  working environment, 12–13
  work schedule, 12

Congressional Management Foundation, 25

Congressional offices, 3–9
  answering mail, 8–9
  budget, 6–7
  casework, 8
  committee offices, 7
  constituents' dominant role, 4–6
  legislative work of (Washington office), 7–8, 9
  personal offices, 7, 8, 9
  representational work of (district or state office), 7, 8–9
  research work of, 9
  small business analogy, 6–7
  staffing
    office management and, 6–7
    research and expertise of, 9
  types of, 7

Congressional Recess, 12

Constituents' dominant role, 4–6
  influence of, 25–26
  listening to constituents, 24

Constitution, U.S., 71–96

Contributors, confidentiality of, vii

Correspondence. *See* Communications; Mail and email

Culture. *See* Congressional culture

D

Davis, Danny, 18–19

Decision-making by legislators, 21–26
  conscience and, 22–23
  flowchart of legislative process, 108
  influences on, 27–34. *See also* Influences on legislative decision-making
  policy research and studying, 23–24
  political aspects of, 24–26

Declaration of Independence, 97–101

DeLay, Tom, 29

Dirksen, Everett, 35

E

Early arrival for meetings, 47

Economic and political footprint, 42–43

Email. *See* Mail and email

Expertise
  of lobbyists, 40
  of staff, 9

F

Face-to-face meetings, 45–54
  acknowledging the legislative "bind" of trying to please everyone, 49–50

Capitol Learning
Audio Courses™

www.CapitolLearning.com

Advocacy Campaigns for Nonprofits
ISBN: 1587330563

Building and Nurturing Your Grassroots Campaign
ISBN: 1587330199

How to Organize a Capitol Hill Day
ISBN: 1587330164

How to Work the Hill Like a Pro
ISBN: 1587330636

Visiting Capitol Hill for First-Time
Grassroots Advocates:
An Introductory Course
ISBN: 1587330555

TheCapitol.Net

Non-partisan training and publications that show how Washington works.™
PO Box 25706, Alexandria, VA 22313-5706   703-739-3790   www.TheCapitol.Net

About TheCapitol.Net

We help you understand Washington and Congress.™

For over 30 years, TheCapitol.Net and its predecessor, Congressional Quarterly Executive Conferences, have been training professionals from government, military, business, and NGOs on the dynamics and operations of the legislative and executive branches and how to work with them.

Our training and publications include congressional operations, legislative and budget process, communication and advocacy, media and public relations, research, business etiquette, and more.

TheCapitol.Net is a non-partisan firm.

TheCapitol.Net encompasses a dynamic team of more than 150 faculty members and authors, all of whom are independent subject matter experts and veterans in their fields. Faculty and authors include senior government executives, former Members of Congress, Hill and agency staff, editors and journalists, lobbyists, lawyers, nonprofit executives and scholars.

We have worked with hundreds of clients across the country to develop and produce a wide variety of custom, on-site training. All courses, seminars and workshops can be tailored to align with your organization's educational objectives and presented on-site at your location.

TheCapitol.Net has more than 2,000 clients representing congressional offices, federal and state agencies, military branches, corporations, associations, news media and NGOs nationwide.

Our blog: **Hobnob Blog—**
hit or miss ... give or take ... this or that ...

**TheCapitol.Net supports the
T.C. Williams Debate Society and the
Scholarship Fund of Alexandria.**

TheCapitol.Net

Non-partisan training and publications that show how Washington works.™
PO Box 25706, Alexandria, VA 22313-5706 703-739-3790 www.TheCapitol.Net

6/11 A

CPSIA information can be obtained at www.ICGtesting.com
227985LV00001B/87/P

9 781587 331817